Copyright © 2021 by KEDO Union Company LTD.

All rights reserved. No part of this book may be reproduced in any form without written permission of the copyright owners, except for a reviewer, who may quote brief passages.

All non-original art and information in this book has been reproduced with the prior consent and/or authorization of sources, and no responsibility is accepted by the producer, publisher, or printer for any infringement of copyright or otherwise, arising from the contents of this publication. Every effort has been made to ensure that credits accurately comply with the information supplied. We apologize for any inaccuracies that may have occurred and will resolve inaccurate or missing information in a subsequent reprinting of this book and all necessary public corrections.

First published in Canada by
KEDO Union Company LTD.
11007 Jasper Ave NW
Edmonton, Alberta T5K 0K6
Telephone: (888) 500-2850
www.kedounion.com

COVER DESIGN
Kate Duke

BOOK DESIGN & LAYOUT
Kate Duke / Canva Pro

To access online content go to www.kedounion.com

Printed in Canada

The information in this book is for informational purposes only. It is not intended to replace the advice of a physician or medical practitioner. Please consult a professional medical care provider before making dramatic lifestyle or nutritional changes.

The Basics of Nutrition 1 : Kid-Friendly

ISBN 978-1-7775347-0-7
ISBN 978-1-7775347-1-4
ISBN 978-1-7775347-2-1

10   9   8   7   6   5   4   3   2   1

THIS BOOK WAS

Written & Designed by

Kate Duke

Edited by

Sophlynda McBetts

Michelle Temple

& KEDO Union Company

and

Colour Art Design by
(your name here)

For our future creations.

Thank you,

Kate Duke

WELCOME TO KEDO

WELCOME TO KEDO KIDS' NUTRITIONAL SERIES

IF YOU ARE READING THIS, IT MEANS THAT YOU HAVE JUST TAKEN A <u>BIG</u> STEP TOWARDS BECOMING A STRONGER AND MORE RESPONSIBLE HUMAN!!

In this book, you will learn the "basics" of nutrition including how it all works, how your body uses what you eat, AND how our Earth and animal neighbours are affected by our demand for food. You will get the information and tools you'll need to make healthier decisions for you and your family, and better choices for your community AND our world; because the truth is..

WE ALL NEED YOU

CHALLENGE YOURSELF

Find tests, games, contests, videos and recipes at

www.kedounion.com/kids

FIND US ON INSTAGRAM

@KedoUnion

Don't forget to tag us in your designs & creations to win prizes and be featured!

-- Psssssst.. --

There might be a lot of new, big and weird words in this book. On pages 6-7, you can find the meaning of most of them, but we might miss one or two! If you don't know what a word means, ask an adult if you can search for it on the internet, then fill it in on page 8 and teach your whole class or family!

CONTENTS

-BASICS-

welcome 3
contents 4
words2know 6
basics of nutrition 10
measuring nutrition 13
14 the rules
16 history of nutrition

-NUTRIENTS-

essential nutrients 18
macronutrients 19
water 20
protein 21
lipids/fat 22
carbohydrates 23
24 dietary fibre
25 micronutrients
26 vitamins
28 minerals
29 non-food sources

-THE BODY-

nutrition & the body 32
anatomy systems 33
digestive system 34
absorption & transport 36
gas 37
hydration 38
40 electrolytes
41 energy
42 nutrition for athletes
44 blood sugar & diabetes

-FOOD-

allergies 46
food production 47
processing 48
how to read a label 49
food groups 50
grains 51
fruits 52
53 vegetables
54 meat
57 what is organic?
58 meals
60 diets
63 secret recipe
66 superfoods

-AROUND THE WORLD-

food culture 68
world issues 70
resources & access 72
sustainability 73
int'l food trade 74
what is fair trade? 75

76 global views
78 impacts on Earth
79 impact on animals
80 the cow
81 the tiger
82 the two-toed sloth

-NUTRITION FOR HEALTH-

nutrition for health 84
nutrition for medicine 86
antioxidants 88
immunity 89
tips & mantras 90

-MINDFUL EATING-

mindful eating 92
food for fuel 93
ABC's of nutrition 94
power of the rainbow 95
tracking nutrition 96
cost of convenience 98

99 making things sweeter
100 more than food
102 healthier choices
104 secret recipes
107 eating responsibly

!KEEP GOING!

As You Grow 113
Be a Composter 114
Be a Cultivator 115
Making Connections 116
Keep Learning 117

118 Upcoming Books
119 Come & Find Us!

WORDS 2 KNOW

ABSORPTION - Process of taking substance into interior body

ARTIFICIAL - Made or produced rather than naturally occurring

ATP - Currency of a cell

BYPRODUCT - An incidental or secondary product made in the production of something else

CATABOLIC PATHWAY - The release of energy trapped in chemical bonds

CHRONIC - Consistently reoccurring

CUISINE - A manner or style of preparing food

DEAMINATION - The removal of an animo group from a molecule

DIGESTION - The process of breaking down substance small enough to digest

ENZYMES - Protein molecules that speed up chemical reactions and remain unchanged

ENERGY YIELDING - (carbs, lipids, proteins) - Provides energy to the body

ENRICHED - Nutrients added to above natural levels

EXCREMENT / FECES - Body Waste - including unabsorbed food residue, bacteria & dead cells

FORTIFIED - Nutrients lost during processing are added back in

GASTROINTESTINAL TRACT (GI TRACT) - Consists of mouth, pharynx, esophagus, stomach, small intestine, large intestine & anus

GENE - Unit of hereditary values; made up of DNA

HOMEOSTASIS - Body regulation
HORMONES - Chemical messengers secreted via blood
HYDROLYSIS / HYDROLYZED - Chemical reaction in which water is added to a substance, potentially gaining Hydrogen
INORGANIC MOLECULES (structure) - Minerals & water
INTUITIVE - Basing on what feels to be true without conscious reasoning
MALNUTRITION - An imbalance in nutrient intake
METABOLIC PATHWAYS - A series of reactions needed to transform food into final product to be used by body
METABOLISM - All bodily reactions
NUTRIGENOMICS - Interaction between genetic variation & nutrition
ORGANIC MOLECULE (structure) - Proteins, lipids, carbohydrates, vitamins
PHYTOCHEMICALS - From plant sources
SECRETE / SECRETIONS - Discharge or product of a cell, gland or organ
TRANSIT TIME - The amount of time to travel GI Tract
ZOOCHEMICALS - From animal sources

ABBREVIATIONS 2 KNOW

AA - Amino Acids
AMDR - Accepted Macronutrient Distribution Range
BMI - Body Mass Index
DV - Daily Value
GI - Gastrointestinal
LI - Large Intestine
MIN - Minerals
RDA - Recommended Dietary Allowance
RMR - Resting Metabolic Rate
SI - Small Intestine
VIT - Vitamin
WW - Whole Wheat

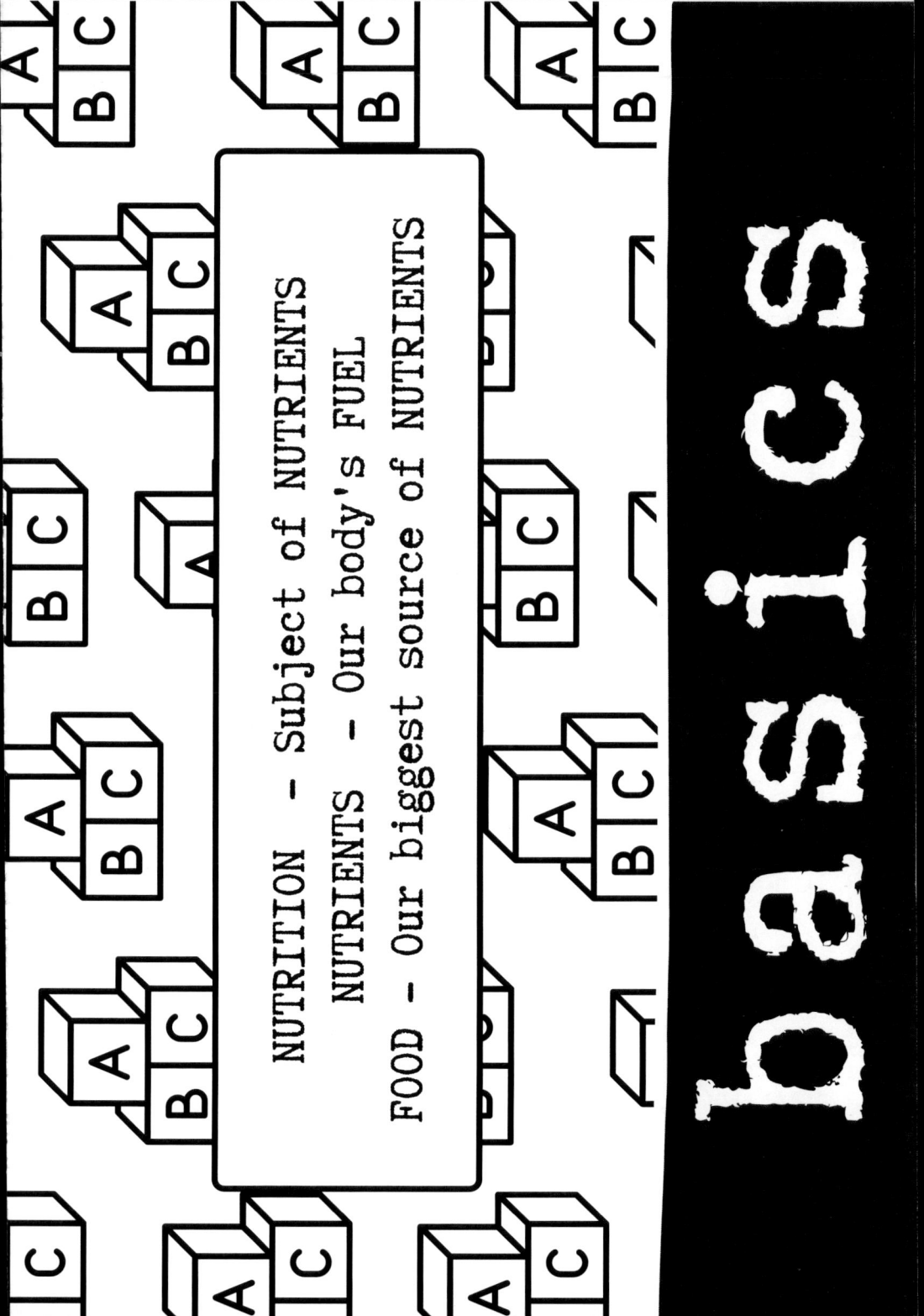

NUTRITION refers to the 'branch' of science that studies the human body, and what it needs to live optimally. Adequate, balanced and fulfilling nutrition (along with air, exercise and love) is key to living a long, strong, and happy life.

NUTRIENTS
AS DEFINED BY OXFORD'S DICTIONARY

"A SUBSTANCE THAT PROVIDES NOURISHMENT ESSENTIAL FOR GROWTH AND THE MAINTENANCE OF LIFE."

Whether you're a human, a puppy or an elephant (and probably even an alien!), you are designed to run best off of nutrients that are pure and clean, and for most Earth-living animals (including humans!), those NUTRIENTS come from 'FOOD'!

Nutrition plays a role in literally EVERY THING YOU DO, from how fast you run, to how well you sleep at night. Your body needs a variety of nutrients for things like energy & strength and to help protect you from invaders like infection & disease.

OPTIMAL NUTRITION

ADEQUATE AMOUNT OF ALL NUTRIENTS YOU NEED TO FUEL LIFE AND THRIVE

IMPORTANT

PLAYING WITH FOOD, INVENTING RECIPES, AND CREATING ADVENTUROUS MEALS WITH YOUR FAMILY IS FUN, AND ENCOURAGED, AND AN IMPORTANT PART OF OUR WORLD'S CULTURES AND SOCIETIES, BUT PLAYING WITH NUTRITION..

THAT IS <u>VERY</u> DIFFERENT.

NUTRITION IS THE BASIS OF HOW OUR BODY'S AND MINDS ARE ABLE TO RUN AND FUNCTION, AND THERE CAN BE VERY DANGEROUS EFFECTS ON YOUR HEALTH IF YOU TRY TO TAKE YOUR NUTRITION INTO YOUR OWN HANDS, WITHOUT ENOUGH EXPERIENCE OR EDUCATION; NOT TO MENTION, YOU MAY HAVE ALLERGIES TO THINGS THAT YOU AREN'T AWARE OF YET! (SEE PAGE 46)

SO..

RESEARCH, LEARN, TALK, TEACH, BUT KEEP ANY NUTRITIONAL EXPERIMENTS UNDER THE GUIDANCE OF A PROFESSIONAL OR A PARENT/GUARDIAN.

MEASURING NUTRITION

YOU'LL FIND NUTRITION MEASUREMENTS IN MANY FORMS, FROM WORDS (LIKE MICRO AND MACRO) TO NUMBERS (LIKE % AND WEIGHTS).

IT'S EASY TO GET OVERWHELMED AT FIRST, SO DON'T BE AFRAID TO DOUBLE CHECK MEANINGS UNTIL YOU ARE FLUENT!

CALORIES (k/CAL)

.. are a unit measurement of ENERGY. When it comes to our nutrition, it tells us how much energy a food provides, but this is far from all you need to know. SEE PAGE 41 FOR MORE INFO

DAILY VALUE (DV)

THE DAILY VALUE (DV) IS FOUND ON EVERY FOOD ITEM YOU PURCHASE AND IS SHOWN IN EITHER A WEIGHT VALUE, OR %. THIS DV IS BASED OFF OF THE RDA (RECOMMENDED DIETARY ALLOWANCE), WHICH GIVES GUIDELINES (BASED ON AVERAGES), TO HELP ENSURE YOU ARE GETTING THE RIGHT AMOUNT OF NUTRIENTS A DAY. SEE PAGE 49 FOR MORE

METABOLISM

..is all bodily reactions, including the rate/speed in which your body digests nutrients. Everyone's is different, & is affected by genes, lifestyle, & quality of nutrients - SEE PAGE 41.

LOW TO HIGH

TRACE ⟶ MICRO ⟶ MACRO

DEFICIENT ⟶ ADEQUATE ⟶ EXCESS

EMPTY CALORIES ⟶ NUTRIENT-DENSE

MALNOURISHED ⟶ NOURISHED

GLYCEMIC INDEX — SEE PAGE 44

THINGS TO REMEMBER

LIMITATIONS & VARIABLES
Nutrition has many inconsistent factors including:

FOOD
Size, ripeness, production, and preparation all affect the nutrients in our food, so values can never be guaranteed

PEOPLE
We are all as different on the outside as we are on the inside. Health, fitness and genetics can all play a role in our nutrition

SCIENCE
The science of nutrition is quite new, so research and studies are often limited and short term

QUALITY
The quality of your nutrition greatly depends on the quality of your food. The best nutrients will come from fresh, whole foods; meaning foods that have no other additives or processing, and that were harvested at the right time, & with minimal time between harvest and your plate.

versus

QUANTITY
It is important to have balance, moderation and variety in all parts of your life; nutrition included. Too much or too little of anything can have short and long term effects. These can range from temporary bloating or indigestion to more scary things like heart problems.

THE BASIS OF LIVING THINGS
With the way humans live and eat, it is very easy to forget that we are just like every other living thing around us. We are creatures of Earth, and, despite our luxuries and "advanced" society, we are not that different from wild animals or even plants. What we need for life is fundamentally the same. For example, a plant needs good quality (& enough) soil, water, air and sunlight to grow, and has absorption & transportation systems to get nutrients around!

WHO MAKES THE RULES

 ## CANADA

HEALTH CANADA

"..responsible for establishing standards for the safety and nutritional quality of all foods sold in Canada. The department exercises this mandate under the authority of the Food and Drugs Act and pursue its regulatory mandate under the Food and Drug Regulations."

CFIA (Canada Food Inspection Authority)

"All health and safety standards under the Food and Drug Regulations are enforced by the Canadian Food Inspection Agency. The Agency is also responsible for the administration of non-health and safety regulations concerning food packaging, labelling and advertising."

www.canada.ca

USA

FDA

CFSAN (Center for Food Safety & Applied Nutrition)

www.fda.gov

 # THE RULES

MAY 4, 2016, HEALTH CANADA, CFIA AND FDA SIGNED AN AGREEMENT RECOGNIZING THEIR FOOD SAFETY SYSTEMS AS COMPARABLE. SIMILAR AGREEMENTS EXIST WORLDWIDE, LIKE AUSTRALIA & NEW ZEALAND, AND THE UK & PARTS OF EUROPE.

THE BASIC PURPOSE OF ALL THESE SYSTEMS ARE THE SAME: TO SET AND ENFORCE STANDARDS AND RULES IN ORDER TO PROTECT THE GENERAL POPULATION (US!)

THE RULES COVER ALL STAGES OF "FOOD PRODUCTION" FROM CULTIVATION THROUGH TO A PRODUCT'S SALE. ALTHOUGH MOST OF THESE RULES ARE SET OUT TO ENSURE WE HAVE TRUE AND DEPENDABLE INFORMATION (SO THAT WE CAN MAKE THE RIGHT AND EDUCATED CHOICES FOR OUR HEALTH AND BODY), IT ALSO IS IN THE BEST INTEREST OF ALL HEALTH SYSTEMS AND GOVERNMENTS TO HAVE THEM IN PLACE, AS THE HEALTHIER THE GENERAL POPULATION, THE LESS STRESS THERE IS ON OUR HOSPITALS AND HEALTHCARE SYSTEMS.

WHILE THERE ARE THOUSANDS OF RULES AND STANDARDS, WHEN IT COMES TO TRUE INFORMATION FOR "CLEAN & HEALTHY EATING", WE DEPEND ON THE FOLLOWING:

NUTRITIONAL INFORMATION
TRUE INGREDIENTS LIST

and

THE VERY ENFORCED & STRICT RULES FOR CLAIMING A PRODUCT AS A "HEALTH PRODUCT" - THIS VARIES COUNTRY TO COUNTRY

and

ORGANIC CERTIFICATION (P.57) & FAIR TRADE PROGRAMS (P.75)

HISTORY OF NUTRITION

<u>1770</u> - Antoine Lavoisier, the "Father of Nutrition and Chemistry", discovered concept of metabolism (the transfer of food and oxygen into heat and water in the body, creating energy).

<u>Early 1800s</u> - the elements of carbon, nitrogen, hydrogen, and oxygen, the main components of food, were isolated and connected to health.

<u>Early 20th Century</u> - Justus Liebig, Germany, began work in the area of the chemical nature of carbohydrates, fats, and proteins. (later leading to the research into Vitamins)

<u>1912</u> - Casimir Funk, a Polish doctor, coined the term "vitamins"

<u>1912</u> - E.V. McCollum, University of Wisconsin, found the first fat-soluble vitamin, Vitamin A.

<u>1919</u> - In the US, the Public Health Service began staffing dieticians in hospitals after Nutrition became globally accepted as having a major role in health.

<u>1929</u> - Professor Sir Frederick Gowland Hopkins wins the Nobel Prize in Physiology or Medicine for the discovery of vitamins, by showing that rats needed more than just a diet of pure proteins, carbohydrates, fats, minerals and water to grow, meaning foods must contain additional unidentified substances for survival needs.

<u>1986</u> - Professor David Barker and his team discovered the relationship between poor nutrition in the womb, birth weight and the lifetime risk of chronic diseases such as coronary heart disease, high blood pressure, stroke and diabetes.

As you can see, the science of food and nutrition is very new (in a lot of ways, not much older than the invention of televisions!).. so new things are being discovered daily, each proving the importance of good quality nutrition for good quality of life!!

ESSENTIAL NUTRIENTS

ESSENTIAL NUTRIENTS are nutrients that your body cannot make itself (or cannot make enough of), but that it needs for basic survival. So far, 45 nutrients have been deemed "essential", and we depend on our diet to get them all, which is just one of the reasons it is so important to have abundance & variety with your food choices!

Essential nutrients have been broken down into the following categories:

Macronutrients
largely needed (quantity)

- Proteins
- Carbohydrates
- Lipids (Fats)
- Water (see page 20)
- Dietary Fibre

 (see page 24)

Micronutrients
small-y needed (quantity)

- Vitamins
- Minerals

SUBSTANTIAL nutrients
... are non-essential nutrients that still benefit life. In other words, a nutrient that benefits your health, but you don't NEED for basic survival.

IT'S ALL CONNECTED
Every nutrient depends on another in some form; whether its anatomical or physiological. A deficit in one nutrient can have multiple negative effects on the short term and long term functions of another. It's kind of amazing if you think about it, but is also a BIG reason you should never adjust your nutrient intake without the guidance of a professional or caregiver!

'MACRO' NUTRIENTS

Macronutrients are nutrients that our body's need in larger quantities. These quantities can depend on a number of factors, including age, height, weight, and any health limitations. The 'AMDR' (Acceptable Macronutrient Distribution Range) was created to provide guidelines on how you should be dividing your daily food intake between the 3 energy providing macronutrients: Protein, 'Carbs' and Lipids. (See page 4I for Nutritional Energy)

PROTEIN
- 10-35% OF AMDR
- Forms ligaments & tendons
- 4 kCal/g
- Needed for growth & maintenance
- Proteins are made up of Amino Acids

CARBOHYDRATES
- aka. "Carbs"
- 45-60% of AMDR
- 4 kCal/gram
- Readily available source of energy
- Includes SUGAR (simple carbs) & STARCHES (complex carbs)

LIPIDS
- aka. "Fats"
- 20-35% of AMDR
- 9 kCal/gram
- Triglycerides - most abundant
- Monounsaturated & poly's - 'GOOD'
- Saturated fatty acids - 'BAD'
- Cholesterol is a type of lipid

WATER
- VITAL for life
- Is both a FOOD and a NUTRIENT
- Not a good source of energy

DIETARY FIBRE
- Debated as a 'macronutrient'
- Not a good source of energy
- Vital for digestion

WATER

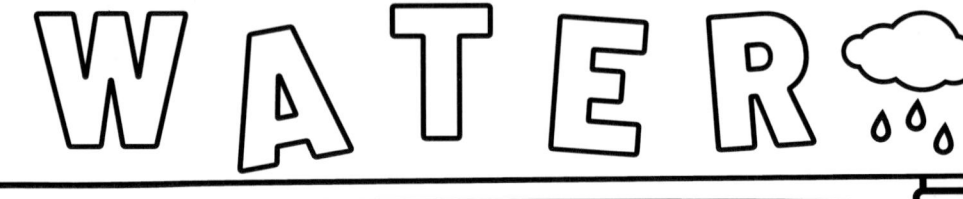

Water is ESSENTIAL to human health and growth, and despite the plentiful supply that we are blessed to have in most first world countries, most of us do not consume enough. Depending on your size, age, and activity level, it is suggested that you should consume a minimum DAILY amount of 0.5-1.0 ounces of water per pound of your total weight. This means (for the average person) if you weigh 100lbs, you should be drinking at least 50oz-100oz of water per day. How do you measure up?

At the time of birth, about 75% of your body mass is water, which slowly decreases to around 50% in your senior years; with the healthy adult body being between 60% & 70%. Lean muscle holds more water than fat, so men typically have slightly more, and this also explains why your water content decreases as you age. Most of your body's water is 'Intracellular' (within your cells), while about 1/3 is 'Extracellular' (outside your cells), and all play vital roles in keeping your body alive and thriving; so it makes sense that any deficit can have very bad consequences to your well-being, both short term and long term. See Page 38 & 39 for more about the roles of water in your body.

APPROXIMATE WATER CONTENT IN PERCENTAGES

- Brain - 75%
- Muscle - 75%
- Bone - 22%
- Blood - 83%
- Skin - 65%

NUTRIENT VS FOOD

Whilst we all know that water is an essential nutrient, the argument that Water should be considered a food is hard to dispute, because.. both are true! Do you know why? While water is a nutrient, we know that a 'food' item is something that <u>provides</u> you nutrients; because water contains multiple minerals, it is, by definition, a food AND a nutrient!

TAKE THE TIME

..to learn about the impact of water bottles (and other waste) on our oceans by researching:

<u>The Great Pacific Garbage Patch</u>

PROTEIN

PROTEIN IS COMMMONLY UNDERSTOOD AS THE 'TOUGH GUY' MACRO, AND IN MANY REGARDS, IT IS. ASIDES FROM IT'S ENERGY-YIELDING PROPERTIES, TOUGHNESS IS INTERTWINED INTO MANY OF IT'S MOST VITAL FUNCTIONS (SEE BELOW). WHAT IS MISUNDERSTOOD, HOWEVER, IS THE IMPORTANCE OF QUALITY OVER QUANTITY; FOR A MULTITUDE OF REASONS. QUALITY: PROTEINS ARE BUILT UP OF CHAINS OF AMINO ACIDS (AA), AND THE QUALITY OF A PROTEIN IS IN IT'S ABILITY TO PROVIDE MULTIPLE AA'S; A COMPLETE PROTEIN BEING NAMED FOR PROVIDING ALL 9 ESSENTIAL AA'S. QUANTITY: EXCESS PROTEINS CAN BE CONVERTED AND STORED AS FAT & CAN LEAD TO WATER LOSS.

WHY DO WE NEED IT

- Provides structure
- Helps regulate fluid & acid balances
- Aids in hormone regulation
- Combines with Vit & Min to speed up/slow down metabolic reactions
- Vital part of immune system (skin & antibodies)
- Moves substances in & out of cells
- Aids in muscular structure & movement

Note: The shape of a protein is what defines it's function.

AMINO ACIDS

- are the building blocks of protein
- can be found in soy (most abundant) & animal proteins
- can be 'deaminated' or repurposed in function
- are part of a constantly working 'Amino Acid Pool'
- There are 9 AA's that the body cannot produce. These must be ingested, or the body will be forced to break down proteins stored in muscles to obtain them.

WHERE DO WE GET IT

PLANT SOURCES
There is an abundance of protein available from plant sources, but are typically in less digestible forms than meat protein.

ANIMAL SOURCES
Meat is probably the first thing you think of when it comes to protein. If you do choose meat, try to choose leaner sources like turkey & chicken.

SUPPLEMENTS
Protein Shakes (etc.) have become widely consumed and come in a variety of both animal and plant forms. They are NOT meant as your main source of protein.

MYTHBUSTER

HUMANS NEED MEAT TO GET ADEQUATE PROTEIN
(see page 54)

LIPIDS (aka 'fats')

Lipids (or 'fats') are likely one of nutrition's most misunderstood terms; not only are lipids VITAL to our existence, but they are also one of the most valuable keys to elevated. While you may recognize visible fat on your body as a negative health indicator, it is not always parallel to your lipid intake, as there can be a number of factors contributing to excess bodily fat ratio (BMI. See Page 4I). A trick is to try to mentally separate "fat" into two topics: 'fat on the body as storage' & 'fat as a functioning nutrient'. Although an excess of lipids will store in the form of bodily fat if not metabolized, certain lipids are known to be associated with an increased BMI. It is, however, ESSENTIAL that we consistently consume & store fat, as not only does it have many physiological roles that cannot efficiently be reproduced (see below), but stores are vital to optimal energy metabolization (see page 4I). Fats are formed of chains of fatty acids, with length defining function. The four major fat groups are predominantly grouped by the number of bonds or molecules it has in its chain: Saturated (not yet bonded), Monounsaturated (one bond), Polyunsaturated (multiple bonds), Trans (double bonds).

USES OF FAT IN THE BODY

- Defines shape
- Stored energy
- Insulates body
- Protects organs
- Lubricates body surfaces (mucous, eye membrane)
- Nutrient transporter
- Essential in micronutrient function
- Principle compound in cellular membranes
- Plays vital role in estrogen regulation
- Some types used as a form of detergent

CRITICAL IN NERVOUS SYSTEM'S FUNCTIONS & SIGNALS.

'GOOD' VS 'BAD'

There are many different types & functions of fat in our food & body, some great and some dangerous. Consuming 'good fats' are proven to have multiple positive effects on longevity & quality of life; including proven reduction in risk of cancer & heart disease, whereas others can actually increase these risks. The "trick" to lipid consumption (no shock here) is in it's RATIO and not in it's quantity; whereby no fats should be eliminated, and none should be consumed in excess. Choosing to have your fat sources from WHOLE foods will always be the best choice for your overall health, as this will be easier for your body to metabolize and also to ensure you know what you are consuming; but generally speaking, try to choose mono or poly unsaturated fats.

GOOD SOURCES

soy - salmon - trout - sole - swordfish - flax seed - nut oils - seed oils - walnuts - avocado - sunflower seeds - coconut - legumes - whole grains - dairy - lean beef - corn ..

CARBOHYDRATES

THE CARBOHYDRATE GROUP COVERS SUGARS, STARCHES & FIBRES; EACH DEFINED BY THEIR CHAINS & THE BONDS WITHIN THEM. THE CARB'S MOST ESSENTIAL ROLE IS TO PROVIDE THE BODY WITH ENERGY IN THE FORM OF GLUCOSE (PG 41 & 42), AND FOR IT'S DIGESTIVE ROLES & FUNCTIONS. EXCESS CARBS ARE STORED IN THE LIVER & MUSCLES AS GLYCOGEN.

ROLES OF CARBS
- LINING OF CELLS
- ENERGY (SOME CELLS PREFER GLUCOSE FOR ENERGY LIKE RED BLOOD CELLS)
- BLOOD SUGAR REGULATION
- AIDS IN DIGESTION
- BRAIN & NERVE FOOD

TYPES OF CARBS

SIMPLE CARBS
- Sugars
- Shorter chains
- Quickly digested

COMPLEX CARBS
- Starches & Fibre
- Ultimately mono-di-poly
- the digestion of carb's reduces the number of bonds for absorption.

LOW CARB DIETS

LONG TERM EFFECTS	SHORT TERM EFFECTS
WEIGHT LOSS	HEART DISEASE
-	-
-	COLON CANCER
METABOLIC BENEFITS	-
-	INFLAMMATION
-	-
IMPROVED INSULIN SENSITIVITY	INSULIN RESISTENCE

OPTIMAL CARBOHYDRATE SOURCES

CHOOSE WHOLE GRAINS
THIS INCLUDES ALL 3 LAYERS OF THE GRAIN: BRAN LAYERS (FIBRE & VITS), ENDOSPERM (STARCH & PROTEIN) AND THE GERM (VIT E & VEGETABLE OILS).

'REFINING' REMOVES ALL BUT ENDOSPERM

bananas - oats - quinoa - sweet potato - buckwheat - oranges - cornmeal - brown rice - corn - kiwi - kidney beans - sunflower seeds - peanut butter - spaghetti - yoghurt - milk - carrot - WW bread

...what is... 'DIETARY FIBRE'

Dietary Fibre:
- is naturally occurring
- comes from our food
- has physiological benefits to our health
- are edible carbs that are not 'hydrolyzed' by our small intestines
- is vital to digestion
- has 'binding' and 'bulking' properties
- has 'water-holding' capacity
- 'Soluble Fibre' is soluble in water and can be found in oats, beans & apples. Insoluble fibre can be found in bran & fruit/vegetable peels.

'THE FIBRE GAP'
This is the name given by researchers to the current state of dietary fibre intake within our population. Research shows that both men and women, in all age ranges, are deficient in this intake. Studies in the diets of our ancestors, in both North America and Australia, are finding humans today are consuming 4-10 times less dietary fibre than humans that dwelled in caves. With nutritional research so new, we are now starting to learn the links & importance of adequate dietary fibre intake for our health. It is believed by many now that Dietary Fibre belongs with the Macros!

WHAT DOES YOUR POOP TELL YOU?
Your poop (or feces/stool) can be one of the biggest indicators of your nutritional health. Adequate water and fibre intake is essential to good digestion and stool; which should be brown in colour, log shaped, and shouldn't disintegrate (fall apart) when you flush. Stool that is watery, a different colour, or painful to pass could indicate something is wrong, especially if it is black or red, so let a parent know if you are experiencing these.

Note: it's important to know that the 'Total Fibre' on nutritional labels (page 49), is both 'Functional Fibre' and 'Dietary Fibre'

'MICRO' NUTRIENTS

THE TERM MICRO MEANS SMALL, SO 'MICRO NUTRIENTS' ARE: NUTRIENTS NEEDED IN SMALL AMOUNTS. SOME ARE NEEDED IN LARGER QUANTITIES THAN OTHERS, BUT ALL HAVE MAJOR ROLES IN YOUR GROWTH AND HEALTH MAINTENANCE THROUGHOUT LIFE.

MACRO NUTRIENTS HAVE BEEN BROKEN DOWN INTO THE FOLLOWING CATEGORIES:

V I T A M I N S
- FAT SOLUBLE
- WATER SOLUBLE

M I N E R A L S
- MAJOR MINERALS
- TRACE MINERALS

No matter how small the "amount" needed, the duties of vitamins and minerals are HUGE. Each has more than one job, and all are ultimately 'coworkers'; affecting all other nutrients, systems and reactions within your body. Your bones, for example, need multiple micronutrients for optimal health, including Calcium, Vitamin D, Phosphorus, Vitamin A, Magnesium, Fluoride, Vitamin C, & Zinc. Consuming Micro nutrients in correct proportions is very important, as an excess in one can create an inability to process another, and can even mask imbalances or deficits. Micronutrients are not sources of energy, but rather AID in the processing of energy from Lipids, Proteins, and Carbs. Minerals are needed primarily for bone strength, nerve transmission & impulses, and transportation of oxygen.

VITA

Fat Soluble (stored in Fat)

VITAMIN	SOURCE
A	Animal organ meat, sweet potato, spinach, dairy, peppers, mango, broccoli, fortified cereals, US!
D	Sunshine, oily/fatty fish (salmon, sardines, herring etc), egg yolks, fortified cereals
E	Wheat germ oil, sunflower seeds, almonds, nut butter, sunflower oil, kiwi, spinach, broccoli
K	Dark leafy greens (collard, spinach, kale etc), broccoli, pomegranate, blueberries, nuts, pumpkin

- REPLENISHMENT -

Water soluble vitamins must be replenished (stocked up on) daily, as they dissolve easily in the blood stream, and any excess is lost through your urine. Fat soluble vitamins are stored in fat, so they can build up and cause toxicity if taken in excess long term (usually from supplement consumption).

VITAMINS

VITAMIN	SOURCE
Thiamin (B1)	Enriched grains, legumes, nuts & seeds
Riboflavin (B2)	Mushrooms, broccoli, whole grains, fish
Niacin (B3)	Added to enriched flour in North America
Biotin	Eggs, seeds, nuts, fish, sweet potato
Pantothenic Acid	Mushrooms, avocado, broccoli
Vitamin B6	Bananas, oats, peanuts, soya beans, poultry
Folate	Leafy greens, chickpeas, liver, brussel sprouts
Vitamin B12	Fish, eggs, milk, cheese, poultry, cereal
Vitamin C	Citrus fruits, apples, broccoli, peppers
Choline	Red meat, fish, poultry, eggs, brussel sprouts

Water Soluble (dissolves in water)

AS MORE RESEARCH IS INVESTED IN OUR FOOD & NUTRITIONAL NEEDS, WE ARE LEARNING MORE ABOUT THE ROLES & RELATIONSHIPS THEY HAVE WITHIN OUR BODY. ESSENTIAL NUTRIENTS AND THEIR BEST SOURCES COULD CHANGE AT ANY TIME, SO TRY TO STAY AS UP TO DATE AS YOU CAN BY REMEMBERING TO READ & RESEARCH NUTRITIONAL INFORMATION LABELS! (PAGE 49)

MINE

MAJOR MINERALS	SOURCES
CALCIUM	Milk & alternatives, fish with bones, tofu, legumes, dark green veggies, sesame seeds
PHOSPHORUS	Found in almost all foods, it is even added to processed foods. Deficiency is very rare
MAGNESIUM	Cashews, soy, sesame & pumpkin seeds, leafy greens. Involved in 600+ chemical functions
SODIUM	Most diets are in excess of sodium. Found in processed & canned foods, bread & seasonings
POTASSIUM	Banana, melon, broccoli, spinach, avocado, sweet potato, dates, prunes, beets, beans
CHLORIDE	Tablesalt, seasalt, seaweed, celery, tomato, lettuce, olives. Deficiency is very rare.
SULFUR	There are many food and non-food sources of Sulfur, including vitamins Thiamin & Biotin

MAJOR MINERALS are minerals that you need in amounts GREATER than 100mg per day, or more than 0.01% of your body weight.

RALS

TRACE MINERALS — SOURCES

IRON — Animal protein (meat), iron cookware, fish, dark leafy greens, most cereals, dried fruit, beans

MANGANESE — Whole grains, nuts, black pepper, coffee, tea, spices, oysters, leafy greens, pineapple, acai

COPPER — Animal organ meat (liver etc), seafood, dark chocolate, nuts, seeds, whole grain foods

IODINE — Iodine content of foods depends on soil of plants & grazing animals. Closer to the Ocean = more Iodine

ZINC — Fortified foods, legume juices, nuts, cereal grains, potatoes, animal proteins, beans, dairy

CHROMIUM — Brewer's yeast, animal organ meat, whole grains, nuts, stainless steel cookware, grape & orange juice

FLUORIDE — Present in small amounts in almost all types of soil, water, plants, animals. Some non-food sources

SELENIUM — Brazil nuts, tuna, shrimp, halibut, animal organ protein, animal protein, whole grain, dairy, beans

---

TRACE MINERALS are required in very small amounts: UNDER 100mg a day, or less than 0.1% of your body weight!!

This is not a complete list! How many others can you find?!

By now, you might have already noticed that food is NOT our only source of Nutrition! We can get Vitamin D from sunshine, Iron from cookware, and there are many non-food sources of Fluoride! Artificial forms of supplements are also on the market, and health professionals use a variety of methods and sources to meet a range of nutritional needs.

SUPPLEMENTS

You've probably already seen some form of supplements around your home, on the television, or at your local store! They usually do not require a prescription, but you should only take supplements under the guidance of a parent or professional; they might look like fun teddy bears or cartoons, but they can also have harmful effects.

NON-FOOD SOURCES OF NUTRITION

MEDICAL INTERVENTION

Medical intervention could be needed for a number of reasons, and administered in many ways. A doctor could prescribe something that alters a chemical reaction (directly or indirectly), recommend diet changes, or, in cases when a patient cannot eat or digest food themselves, medical professionals can provide nutrition by way of Alternative Feeding Methods.

Common Reasons for Medical Intervention:

- Pregnancy
- Lifestyle changes
- Side effects from med
- Genetics
- Illness
- Age

ALTERNATIVE FEEDING

'Tube feeding' - Enternal - Nasogastric - Gastronomy - Intravenous - Total Parental Nutrition - Supplementation -

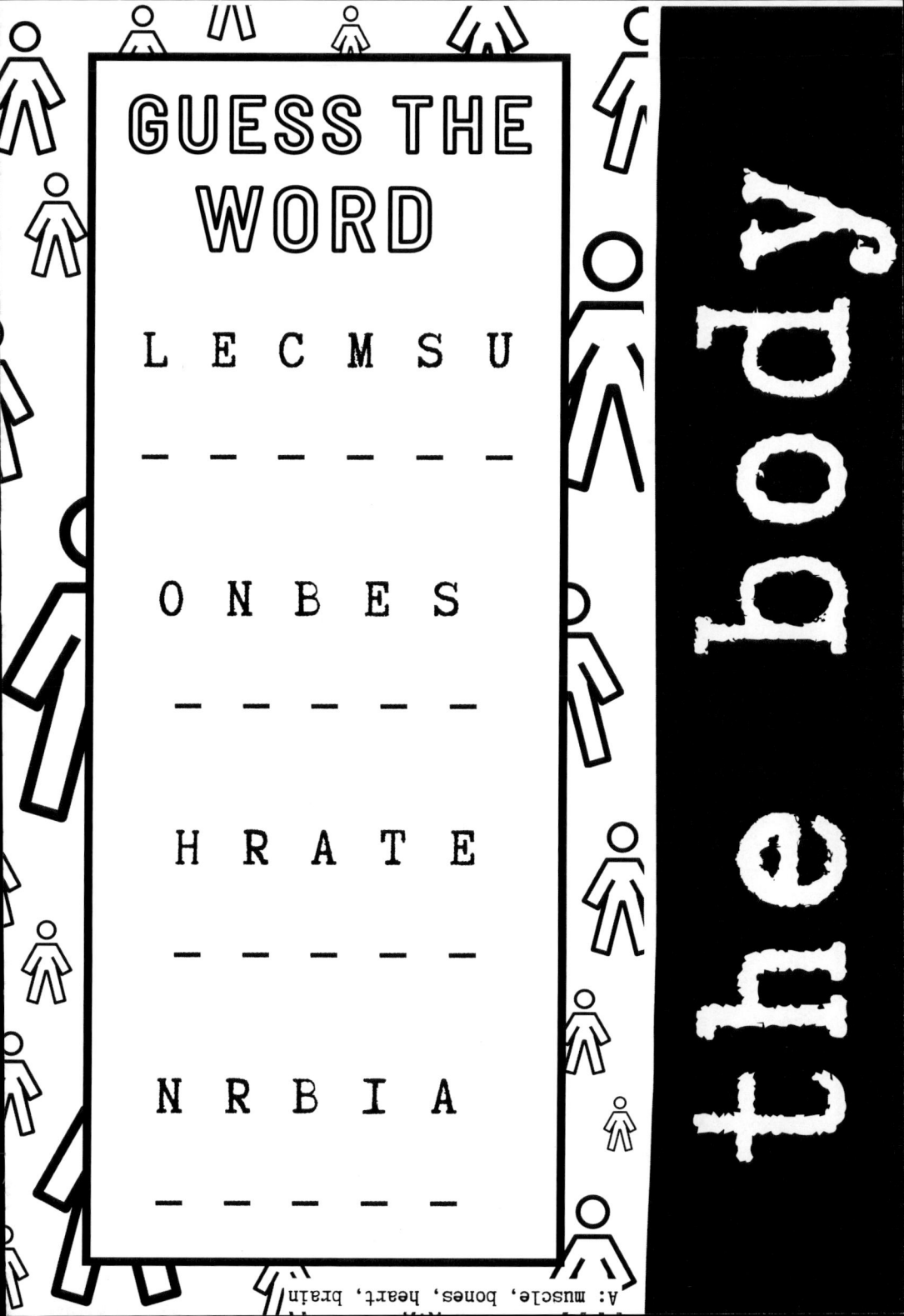

NUTRITION & ANATOMY

Anatomy is the branch of science that covers the physical aspect of your body's STRUCTURE. Everything is connected through multiple organ and transport systems (see pg 93), each working both independently & collaboratively for optimal health. There is so much to learn about anatomy and it's relationship with nutrition, so today we will focus on how the digestive, transport & absorption systems work. You'll be able to build on this knowledge as you work through the rest of the book, and as you continue to learn through your own life, schooling & KEDO.

NUTRITION & PHYSIOLOGY
(fizzy-ology)

Physiology is the branch of science that covers your body's FUNCTIONS; this includes interactions, processes and methods of self-regulation. It's physiology that gives you the signals of hunger, sleepiness, thirst & even love, but it does the greatest of it's work without you even knowing. Your temperature, hormone balance, enzyme secretions, nerve signals & reactions, mood and immunity functions are just a few of the systems that subconsciously work around the clock.

Physiological reactions in your body can be affected by many factors:

- Genes
- Nutrition/hydration
- Environment
- Medication
- Physical Activit
- Stress

ORGAN SYSTEMS

YOU are an ORGANISM, made up of multiple ORGAN SYSTEMS; which is made up of multiple ORGANS; which is made up of multiple TISSUES; which is made up of multiple CELLS; which is made up of multiple MOLECULES; which is made up of multiple ATOMS!!

NERVOUS SYSTEM
brain, spinal cord, nerves

URINARY SYSTEM
kidneys, bladder, & associated structures

CARDIOVASCULAR
heart & blood vessels

MUSCULAR SYSTEM
skeletal muscles

INTEGUMENTARY
skin, hair, nails, sweat glands

RESPIRATORY SYSTEM
lungs, trachea, air passage ways

REPRODUCTIVE SYS.
testes, ovaries, & associated structures

LYMPHATIC/IMMUNE
lymphs, white blood cells

SKELETAL SYSTEM
bones, joints

ENDOCRINE SYSTEM
pituitary, adrenal, thyroid, pancreas & other ductless glands

DIGESTIVE SYSTEM
mouth, pharynx, esophagus, stomach, small & large intestines, pancreas, liver & gall-bladder

digestive

mouth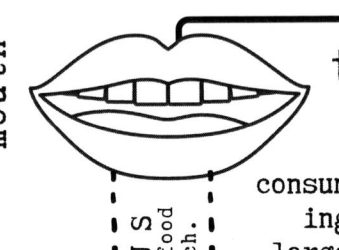

teeth
Teeth begin the process of food consumption by breaking it down into a larger surface area.

saliva
Saliva aids in digestion by both adding moisture, but it also contains amylase, which begins the break down of Carbs.

ESOPHAGUS contracts, pushing food bolus towards stomach.

pharynx
The pharynx is located at the back of your throat, and is responsible for swallowing food & sending it into the esophagus as 'bolus'.

— TO STOMACH

stomach
The stomach mixes & churns up food, and secretes stomach acid & protein-digesting enzymes. It has sphincters located at each end, which open and close to allow food to pass through. It has 3 different layers of smooth muscles, (longitudinal, circular & diagonal), which work together for maximum mixing power! Now, onto the INTESTINES!!

THE 'TUBE' THAT RUNS FROM YOUR MOUTH THROUGH YOUR DIGESTIVE ORGANS & DOWN TO YOUR ANUS IS CALLED YOUR GASTROINTESTINAL TRACT

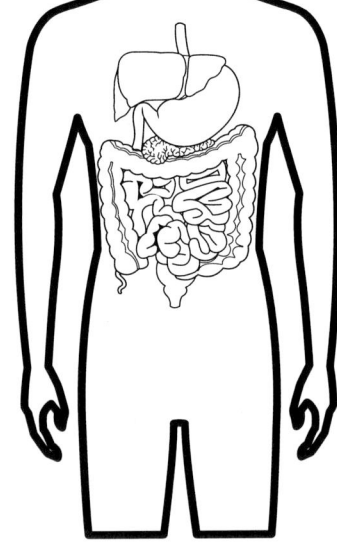

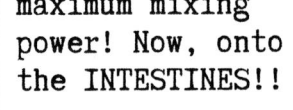

system

ENDOCRINE SYSTEM

LIVER
..produces bile, which is needed for fat digestion absorption. Bile is then secreted into the gallbladder for storage. The liver has MANY jobs!

PANCREAS
When triggered by CCK, the pancreas releases pancreatic juices (a bicarbonate), which neutralizes intestinal contents, while also producing the enzymes needed to further digest macros.

GALL BLADDER
Secretes bile; produced in the liver, and is then stored in the gallbladder.

INTESTINES

SMALL INTESTINE
The small intestine is a long, hallow tube that runs from the end of your stomach, to the entrance of your Large Intestine. The inside of the small intestine is lined with folds, which are coated with microvilli; filtering nutrients into either the bloodstream or lymphs.

LARGE INTESTINE
..does not participate in 'digestion' of nutrients, as all but dietary fibre are absorbed within the small intestine. The L.I. contains the colon and rectum & is responsible for carrying all waste through as excrement. The L.I also contains bacterial enzymes, (good gut bacteria) and absorbs needed water.

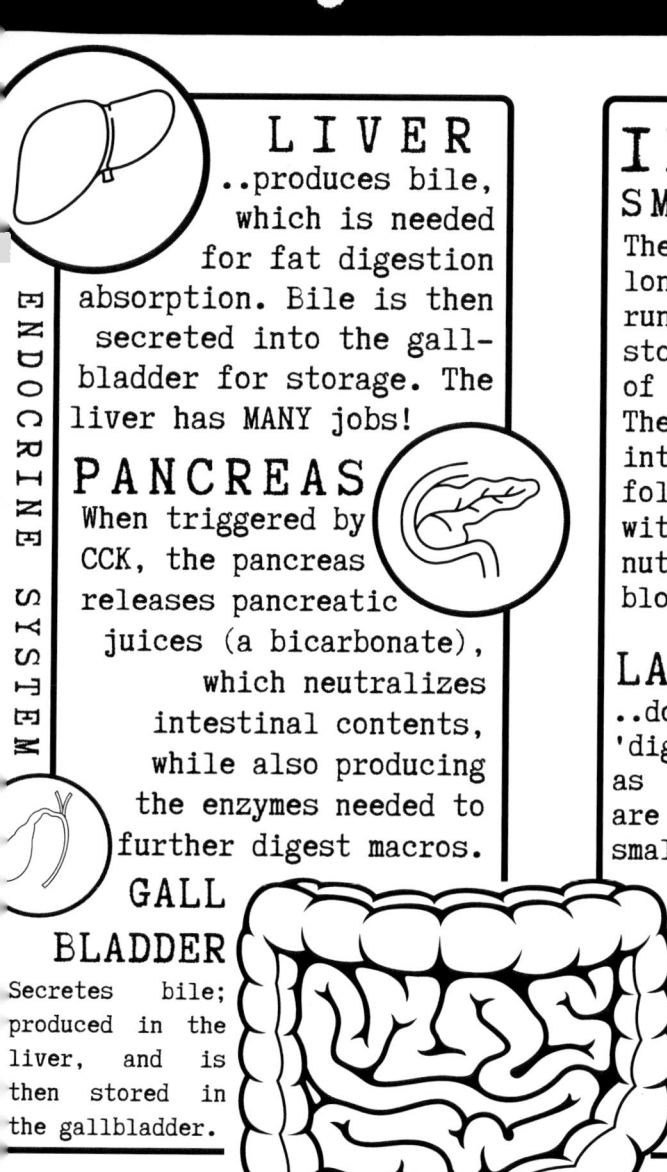

ANUS
Opens to allow waste to exit body

GI TRACTS' ROLE IN OUR IMMUNITY
Limits absorption of toxins & disease-causing organisms - some immunity cells reside in GI Tract to fight antigens (see page 89).

ABSORPTION & TRANSPORT

ABSORPTION
THE PROCESS OF TAKING IN SUBSTANCES TO THE INTERIOR BODY..

The process of digestion breaks food down into substances small enough for the body to absorb for transport; which typically means breaking the bonds within the chains of macronutrients and the release of micronutrients from within the food itself.

Most absorption of the nutrients in our food happens within the small intestine, although some does happen in the stomach. The SI is lined with multiple folds coated in villi, which look somewhat like long feelers. On each waving villi are smaller microvilli, which are nutrient-specific & are responsible for absorption.

NOTE: The nutrient-specific receptors are essential to the process, as absorption methods vary by nutrient.

TRANSPORT
THE PROCESS OF MOVING NUTRIENTS AROUND THE BODY AS NEEDED..

BLOODSTREAM

Most nutrients are transported around the body through the blood stream. In the absorption process, nutrients will pass through the wall lining of the SI in (generally) one of two ways. In 'Active Transport Diffusion, nutrients will be carried into the bloodstream by a carrier molecule. In the case of passive absorption, one highly concentrated area will, over time, spread itself into areas of low concentration, much like pouring liquid through cloth.

Once in the bloodstream, nutrients will be distributed to perform their daily functions, many forming reactions as they go. The blood stream also returns any waste to be evacuated (below).

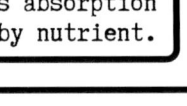

EXCRAMENT
FECES (POOP), URINE (PEE)

Feces - waste including unabsorbed food residue, fibre, bacteria and dead cells.

GAS

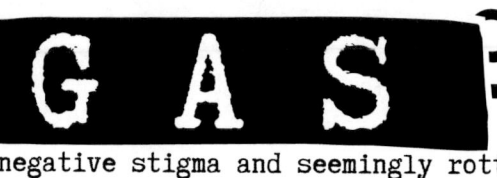

Despite their negative stigma and seemingly rotten range of personalities, the gas family are a natural, well-meaning group, that speak the true universal language. Typically expressing themselves through burps & farts, human created gasses have prevailed over their public perception to continue their very important jobs.

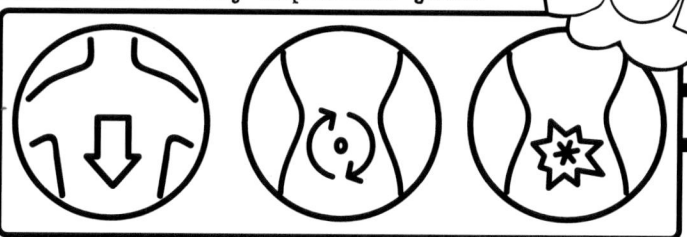

Gas is a necessary bodily function and occurs, in some form, in every living thing. In humans, it is a byproduct of both energy production and food digestion (among other things). Most of the gas you encounter is likely a product of the latter: food digestion. Burps are typically a product of swallowing air, or churning in the stomach, while farts are typically due to gas production in the Large Intestines.

So why does some gas smell SO much worse than others? Our food & drink sources have a lot to do with this, and there are a few that have some fame for their gas quantity or stank power. This can often be chopped up to fermentation of contents (Carbs) in your Large Intenstines. Excess gas can also be brought on by things like intolerances or medications; and while farts & burps can seem like fun & jokes, being gassy can cause a lot of discomfort. Luckily, there are many effective remedies.

HYDRA

ROLES OF WATER IN THE BODY

AS YOU LEARNED ON PAGE 20, WATER IS ESSENTIAL TO LIFE. WATER IS A HEAT REGULATOR, TOXIN CLEANSER, TRANSPORT & PROTECTION SYSTEM, AND IS A CATALYST TO YOUR BODY'S DAILY FUNCTIONS & REACTIONS. WATER IS REQUIRED FOR VIRTUALLY ALL BODILY FUNCTIONS, & MAKES UP A HUGE PERCENTAGE OF YOUR BODY'S VOLUME.

FLUID GAINS AND LOSSES

GAINS
<u>BEVERAGES</u> - 80-90%
<u>FOODS</u> - FRUITS&VEG>
  OILS, GRAINS, MEAT
<u>METABOLIC WATER</u> - MADE
  IN METABOLIC REACTIONS

LOSSES
URINE, SWEAT, LUNGS, FECES
-INFLUENCED BY-
ENVIRONMENT, EXERCISE,
ILLNESS, INJURY, DIURETICS,
PREGNANCY, BREASTFEEDING

---DEHYDRATION---

DEHYDRATION IS OFTEN MEASURED BY ACUTE (SMALL) DECREASE IN BODY WEIGHT (ESPECIALLY IN ATHLETES), AND IT DOESN'T TAKE MUCH TO BEGIN TO FEEL SOME OF THESE EFFECTS; MANY OF WHICH YOU MAY HAVE ALREADY EXPERIENCED, DESPITE OUR AMPLE ACCESS TO FLUIDS.

% OF BODY WEIGHT LOST	SYMPTOMS
1-2%	THIRST, DISCOMFORT, LOSS OF APPETITE
3-5%	NAUSEA, FLUSHED SKIN, LACK OF CONCENTRATION
>8%	DELIRIUM, MUSCLE SPASMS, DEATH

ONE OF THE EASIER, SELF-ADMINISTER-ABLE HYDRATION TESTS IS 'THE PEE COLOUR TEST'. THIS CAN BE DONE THROUGHOUT THE DAY, & CAN BE THE FIRST TELL-TALE SIGN TO INCREASE YOUR WATER INTAKE. SEARCH ON GOOGLE FOR THE CHART (WITH PARENT'S PERMISSION) & SEE HOW YOU MEASURE UP TODAY.. AND TOMORROW!!

...TION!!

mouth

Hydration begins in the mouth before you even fill up your glass! Signals cause dryness in the mouth triggering your thirst; then, drink!

ESOPHAGUS

TO STOMACH

Water travels through the esophagus and into your stomach. It is from there that it then enters your small intestines and is absorbed via cell walls to make it's way into the blood stream. Unlike food, water is not 'digested', or broken down, before absorption, and for that reason, it is very important to consume as much pure and clean water as you can.

Once water enters the blood stream, it is distributed, as needed, around the body to perform necessary functions.

Once daily roles are completed, water will travel to the kidneys where it is used to flush toxins. From the kidneys, it will make it's way to the bladder where it is processed as urine, & stored until you use the bathroom! Only about 20% of the water you consume ends up in your bladder, due to other means of water loss (see page 38).

Your level of hydration determines the rate in which this all happens; with better hydration resulting in faster travel & distribution time, and ultimately more clear & healthy urine.

NOTE: Not all water is absorbed from the small intestine. 75% of your poo is water, so some will go directly to the Large Instestine to perform it's digestion-aiding roles.

39

ELECTROLYTES

You may have heard of electrolytes before; from commercials, athletic pros or even your drink labels at home.. but do you know what they really are? Well we'll let you in on a little secret: most people don't! So get ready, this is your chance to become the teacher!

Electrolytes are mineral salts that dissolve in water, carry charges & are VITAL for your fluid balance. Electrolytes consist of Sodium, Potassium & Chloride, each with life maintaining responsibilities.

POTASSIUM (K+)
RESONSIBILITIES:
- Assists in Sodium functions
- 'Normal' blood level: 3.5-5.0 mmol/L
- Receives signals triggering muscle contraction
- VITAL for Nerve control
- Found inside cells
- Aids in heartbeat regulation

SODIUM (Na+)
RESONSIBILITIES:
- Fluid Balance
- Electrolyte Balance
- Nerve Impulse & Transmission
- Assists in Nutrient Transport
- Blood Volume - increase in Sodium = increase in blood volume
- 'Normal' blood level: 135-145 mmol/L

CHLORIDE (Cl-)
RESONSIBILITIES:
- Assists most Sodium functions, including fluid balance & cellular interactions.
- Hydrochloric Acid production in the stomach
- Assists in Immunity as a feirce bacteria killer

ENERGY

ALTHOUGH WE HAVE BECOME ACCUSTOMED TO VIEW FOOD FOR ITS TASTY & SATISFYING ASSETS, IT IS ESSENTIAL THAT YOU RECOGNIZE THAT FOOD IS NEEDED NOT FOR SATISFACTION, BUT FOR ESSENTIAL ENERGY PRODUCTION AND NUTRITIONAL FULFILLMENT. ENERGY DOES NOT JUST FUEL YOUR DAILY PHYSICAL ACTIVITIES, BUT ALSO YOUR DAY-TO-DAY LIVING, INCLUDING ALL BODILY REACTIONS WITHIN IT. YOUR QUALITY OF NUTRITION HAS VAST INFLUENCE ON YOUR PERFORMANCE IN BOTH (SEE PAGE 93) AND MAXIMUM EFFICIENCY MEANS CONSUMING THE CORRECT RATIO OF NUTRIENTS WITH OPTIMAL TIMING.

ENERGY-WIELDING NUTRIENTS

LIPIDS/FATS	CARBOHYDRATES	PROTEINS
• 9 kCals/g	• 4 kCals/g	• 4 kCals/g
• 37.6 kJoules/g	• 16.7 kJoules/g	• 16.7 kJoules/g
• Energy comes from stores	• Fast-acting	• Excess intake is used for energy
	• Basis of Glucose	

ENERGY & WEIGHT MANAGEMENT

.. go hand-in-hand. Long term effects of energy imbalances will present in a magnitude of ways, including (but certainly not limited to) weight gain/loss and your BODY MASS INDEX (BMI). Your BMI is one of the more basic indicators of health, and is based on the anthropometric measurements of your weight and height. The simplicity of this test means it should never be a sole indicator, but is valuable.

BMI = (LBS X 703) ÷ INCH ÷ INCH

NOTE: <18.5 BMI AND >30 HAVE PROVEN INCREASED HEALTH RISKS.

There are 3 basic types of energy expenditure within the human body.
- Thermal Effect of Food   5-10%
  - Energy used to process food
- Physical Activity   20-35%
  - Movement above 'basal'
- Basal Metabolic Rate   60-70%
  - Energy required to maintain resting functions of body

Factors that affect BMR: Amount of lean tissue, height, age, gender, fasting, growth (incl. pregnancy), thyroid hormones, some medication.

The primary source of energy is glucose in the form of Carbs; which provide a quick energy spike, followed by a crash until glycogen production kicks in. Stored energy sources are in the liver, muscles fatty tissue, and bodily fluids.

NUTRITION FOR ATHLETES

NUTRITION

ATHLETES REQUIRE ABOVE AVERAGE NUTRITION, BECAUSE ABOVE AVERAGE PERFORMANCE IS REQUIRED FROM THEIR BODIES. TO RUN OPTIMALLY, AN ATHLETE NEEDS TO FUEL ENHANCED LEVELS OF SPEED, POWER, INJURY RESILIENCE, RECOVERY & BEYOND. SEE NEXT PAGE.

HYDRATION

DEHYDRATION RISK IS CONSIDERABLY HIGHER IN ATHLETES DUE TO FUELLED WATER LOSSES (SEE PAGE 38). CONSIDERATION MUST BE TAKEN IN REPLENISHING ALL THAT IS LOST, INCLUDING ELECTROLYTE LEVELS. DEHYDRATION IN ATHLETES IS AVOIDED PROACTIVELY ONLY.

TIMING

EATING FOR ATHLETICISM IS A MATTER OF FUEL, HYDRATION & ADEQUATE NUTRIENT INTAKE.

INSTANT ENERGY
EXPLOSIVENESS
1-3 SECONDS
MUSCULAR ATP

THEN

3-5 SECONDS
CREATINE PHOSPHATE STORES

ANAEROBIC ENERGY
SHORT TERM
15 SECONDS - 2 MINUTES
GLUCOSE

AEROBIC ENERGY
LONG TERM
>2 MINUTES
GLUCOSE & FATTY ACID STORES

LOWER INTENSITY, LONGER DURATION
- USES MORE FAT STORES

HIGH INTENSITY, SHORTER DURATION
- USES MORE CARB STORES

ATHLETICISM

PHYSICAL FITNESS IS THE STATE OF BEING CREATED BY THE INTERACTION BETWEEN NUTRITION AND PHYSICAL ACTIVITY, AND INCLUDES:

- CARDIORESPIRATORY FITNESS
- MUSCOSKELETAL FITNESS
- FLEXIBILITY
- BODY COMPOSITION

ATHLETICISM IS ATTAINED WITH LONG TERM, CONSISTENT CHOICES WITH ONE'S NUTRITION, TRAINING & MENTALITY.

THE TRUE TEST OF ATHLETICISM ON A NUTRITIONAL SCALE, IS OF AN ATHLETE'S MUSCLE'S ABILITY TO STORE GLYCOGEN & THEREBY INCREASING ANAEROBIC ENERGY PERFORMANCE & LONGEVITY. NOTE: <u>ONLY</u> ATTAINABLE WITH DEDICATION&DISCIPLINE.

RECOVERY

REST IS ESSENTIAL FOR BOTH PERFORMANCE & LONGEVITY FOR AN ATHLETE. REST IS NEEDED FOR BASIC REPLENISHMENTS OF ENERGY, LIKE CREATINE PHOSPHATE; RECOVERY IS REQUIRED FOR ABOVE AVERAGE REPLENISHMENTS. INCREASED FAT INTAKE IS NECESSARY DURING PERIODS OF HIGH INTENSITY TRAINING, AS THE BODY WILL USE FAT STORES WHILE IN REST. THE RECOVERY PERIOD ALLOWS FOR AS MUCH INVESTMENT IN PERFORMANCE AS PRE-WORK. ADEQUATE RECOVERY REQUIRES 450ml - 675ml WATER INTAKE FOR EVERY LB LOST DURING EXERCISE. SEE NEXT PAGE FOR MORE.

BUILDING AN ATHLETE'S NUTRITIONAL PLAN

THERE ARE MANY VARIABLES TO THE NUTRITIONAL NEEDS OF AN ATHLETE; ON/OFF SEASON & TRAINING REGIMES BEING THE FIRST TO CONSIDER. FAT (STORES) & GLUCOSE (MUSCLES) ARE THE MAIN SOUR-CES OF ENERGY FOR PHYSICAL ACTIVITY, SO IN TIMES OF TRAINING, MUST BE INCREASED TO MAINTAIN WEIGHT & OPTIMIZE PERFORMANCE. ATHLETE 'TYPE' ALSO DICTATES MUCH OF A NUTRITIONAL PLAN. WHILE MOST ATHLETE'S NEEDS ARE SOMEWHAT UNIVERSAL (INCREASE), EACH WILL BENEFIT FROM A CATERED PLAN DEPENDING ON POSITIONAL & PHYSICAL DEMANDS. A GOOD EXAMPLE IS THAT OF FOOTBALL PLAYERS:

QUARTERBACK VS. O-LINEMAN - LINEBACKER VS. KICKER
WIDE RECIEVER VS. RUNNING BACK

TAKE A LOOK BELOW FOR SOME OF THE THINGS TO CONSIDER.

VISION	GENERAL	SPEED
Increase: VIT C, VIT E, ZINC, VIT A, LUTEIN, OMEGA FATTY ACIDS, CAROTENE	Increase: IRON INTAKE CARBS - 60-100G/KG/DAY PROTEIN - 1.2-1.4G/KG/DAY	Increase: NITRATES, CARB INTAKE, VIT D, UNSAT. FATTY ACIDS, MINIMIZE DAIRY PRODUCTS
COMPETITION DAY INCREASE CARB INTAKE 500-1000kCal 2-4hrs prior INCREASE FLUID INTAKE 400-600ml within 2hr POST MEAL/HYDRATION START WITHIN 30MINS; CARB:PROTEIN = 4:1	HIGH-IMPACT Increase: PROTEIN INTAKE-1.3-1.7G/KG/DAY CARB INTAKE - 30-60G/HR DURING TRAINING	FLEXIBILITY Increase: VITAMIN C, CALCIUM, VIT D, MAGNESIUM, VIT B, IRON, ANTI-OXIDANTS, WATER
IMMUNITY Increase: VIT B-6 VIT A VIT D FOLATE, ANTIOX-IDANTS & OMEGA FATTY ACIDS	ALERTNESS Increase: FOLATE, WHOLE GRAIN, IRON, CHOLINE, VIT B, THIAMIN, FOLATE, BIOTIN	INJURY RESERVE Increase: BIOTIN, NIACIN, VIT B, D, A, C, FOLATE, ANTIOX. MIN. LACTOSE INTAKE

BLOOD SUGAR & DIABETES

BLOOD SUGAR

AS YOU LEARNED ON PAGE 41, YOUR BODY USES GLUCOSE FOR ENERGY, AND MAKING SURE YOU HAVE ENOUGH TO SUSTAIN LIFE & ACTIVITIES IS VITAL TO YOUR SURVIVAL! YOUR 'BLOOD SUGAR LEVEL' IS THE MEASUREMENT OF GLUCOSE CONCENTRATION IN YOUR BLOOD STREAM, & SHOULD BE BETWEEN 3-7 MMOL/L. INSULIN & GLUCOGEN HELP TO MAINTAIN THOSE NUMBERS, BUT SOMETIMES THAT SYSTEM CAN FAIL, TYPICALLY RESULTING IN 'DIABETES'.

INSULIN

INSULIN IS CREATED IN THE PANCREAS, AND IS THE BODY'S WAY OF MANAGING GLUCOSE LEVELS IN YOUR BLOOD STREAM. WHEN YOUR GLUCOSE LEVELS GET TOO HIGH INSULIN WILL BRING IT BACK DOWN. COOL, HUH?

GLYCEMIC INDEX

THE 'GLYCEMIC INDEX' IS A RANKING SYSTEM TO SHOW HOW A FOOD ITEM AFFECTS THE 'GLYCEMIC RESPONSE' IN YOUR BODY.

THE 'GLYCEMIC RESPONSE' IS HOW FAST AND HOW HIGH GLUCOSE RISES IN YOUR BODY AFTER CARBS (SUGARS) ARE CONSUMED.

#	DONUT	CHERRIES	ORANGE	WHOLE MILK	ONION
GI	76	22	43	30	10

DIABETES

TYPE 1
AUTOIMMUNE
THE BODY ATTACKS IT'S OWN GLUCOSE-MAKING CELLS, SO IT CANNOT MAKE GLUCOSE OR ENERGY.

TYPE 2
INSULIN RESILIENT
THE BODY CAN CREATE IT'S OWN INSULIN, BUT THE BODY CAN'T RESPOND PROPERLY.

GESTATIONAL
OCCURS DURING PREGNANCY
IN UP TO 10% OF PREGNANCIES, OCCURS IN SECOND OR THIRD TRIMESTER AND GOES AWAY AFTER BIRTH.

FOOD JOKES

Why did the mushroom go to the party?

              because he was a fungi

What do you give to sick lemon?

              lemon-aid

What did the Burger's name their daughter?

              Patty

What do you call a blueberry band practice?

              a jam sesh

ALLERGIES
!!WARNING!!WARNING!!WARNING!!

EVERY SINGLE ONE OF US WILL MOST LIKELY SUFFER FROM AN ALLERGY AT ONE TIME IN OUR LIVES. SOME CAN MAKE YOU ITCHY, SOME CAN MAKE YOUR NOSE RUNNY, SOME CAN BE LIFE THREATENING, BUT ALL ARE EXAMPLES OF..

ALLERGIC REACTIONS

ALLERGIC REACTIONS HAPPEN WHEN YOUR BODY COMES INTO CONTACT WITH SOMETHING NEW AND, SEEING IT AS A THREAT TO YOUR HEALTH, TRIGGERS YOUR OWN, BUILT IN, AUTOMATIC DEFENCE SYSTEM CALLED YOUR 'AUTOIMMUNITY'. IT IS THIS SYSTEM THAT PROTECTS YOU FROM VIRUSES & DISEASES AND THAT KEEPS YOU RESILIENT & STRONG, BUT IT CAN ALSO FALSELY TRIGGER YOUR BODY INTO AN AUTOMATIC RESPONSE, RESULTING IN AN ALLERGIC REACTION. SOME ALLERGIES CAN COME AND GO OVER TIME, OTHERS CAN BE CONTROLLED WITH MEDICINE, AND SOME HAVE SYMPTOMS SO MINOR YOU MIGHT NOT EVEN NOTICE, BUT SOME REQUIRE A LIFELONG COMMITMENT TO MANAGE SAFELY.

HOW TO FIND OUT IF YOU HAVE ALLERGIES

THERE ARE 2 REAL WAYS TO FIND OUT ABOUT YOUR ALLERGIES..

1. FROM A DOCTOR

DOCTORS CAN TEST FOR ALLERGIES IN A FEW WAYS, BUT MOST COMMONLY TOPICALLY (VIA SKIN). THE BIGGEST BENEFIT IS THAT IT IS CONTROLLED, AND THEREFOR SAFER; BUT IT CAN BE EXPENSIVE AND A DOCTOR WILL USUALLY ONLY TEST FOR THE MOST COMMON ALLERGIES, UNLESS OTHERWISE REQUESTED OR INDICATED, WHICH MEANS THIS METHOD ISN'T ALWAYS INCLUSIVE.

2. FROM A REACTION

THE MOST COMMON WAY TO FIND OUT YOU HAVE AN ALLERGY IS BY HAVING AN ALLERGIC REACTION. LUCKILY MOST REACTIONS ARE MINOR AND CONTROLLABLE, BUT OTHERS REQUIRE IMMEDIATE MEDICAL ATTENTION AND CAN BE SERIOUSLY LIFE THREATENING. IT IS VERY LIKELY YOUR PARENTS OR CAREGIVERS WERE READY FOR SUCH A SCENARIO WHEN FEEDING YOU THINGS LIKE PEANUTS OR SHELLFISH FOR THE FIRST TIME.

ANAPHYLACTIC SHOCK

..OR ANAPHYLAXIS IS ONE OF THE MOST DANGEROUS ALLERGIC REACTIONS. THE CHEMICALS RELEASED BY YOUR AUTOIMMUNE RESPONSE CAUSE YOUR BODY TO GO INTO SHOCK; DROPPING YOUR BLOOD PRESSURE, AND CAUSING YOUR AIRWAY TO CLOSE, BLOCKING YOUR BREATHING. IF THIS IS HAPPENING TO OR AROUND YOU, ASK FOR AN <u>EPIPEN</u> AND CALL 911..

STEPS OF FOOD PRODUCTION

CULTIVATION
(cul-tee-vay-tion)

THIS IS THE STAGE OF GROWTH! IT IS BY FAR THE LONGEST STAGE, AND STARTS WITH GETTING LAND READY FOR ANIMALS OR PLANTS, AND ENDS WHEN THE PRODUCT IS FULLY GROWN AND READY FOR HARVEST!!

HARVEST

 WITH ANY CULTIVATED FOOD, HARVEST IS HARD WORK. IT ALMOST ALWAYS REQUIRES BIG EQUIPMENT, TRUCKS AND TRACTORS, AND A LOT OF SWEAT!! THE TIMING OF HARVEST CAN MAKE A BIG DIFFERENCE WITH THE NUTRITIONAL VALUE OF A PRODUCT (SEE PAGE 53).

SALE

THE BRIDGE FROM FARM TO YOUR HOME HAPPENS DURING THE SALE. A CULTIVATOR CAN CHOOSE TO SELL THEIR PRODUCTS THEMSELVES, INDEPENDENTLY OR AT LOCAL MARKETS, BUT MANY FARMS CHOOSE TO SELL DIRECTLY TO A GROCERY STORE, WHO THEN SELL TO YOU.

CONSUMPTION

..AND FINALLY TO YOUR PLATE!! CHOP, MIX, BAKE, SAUTE.. LET YOUR KITCHEN TAKE YOU ON AN ADVENTURE OR ENJOY THOSE FRUITS AND VEGGIES RAW! HOWEVER YOU LOVE YOUR FOOD, DON'T FORGET TO APPRECIATE HOW FAR IT CAME TO GET TO YOU!

!!WARNING!!
BEWARE OF EXTRA STEPS IN YOUR FOOD PRODUCTION

PROCESSING

IT'S RARE TO FIND FOOD AT A GROCERY STORE THAT HASN'T GONE THROUGH SOME FORM OF PROCESSING, AND IN MANY CASES IS NECESSARY, AND CAN EVEN BE BENEFICIAL. MOST FORMS, HOWEVER, ARE THE OPPOSITE, AND IT'S USE IS USUALLY FOR MONETARY GAIN AND NOT CONSUMER WELL-BEING. THIS OFTEN ENTAILS ARTIFICIAL MANIPULATION.

ADDITIVES

ADDITIVES ARE A LOT LIKE THEY SOUND.. THINGS THAT ARE ADDED; BUT IT ALSO SOUNDS A LITTLE LIKE THE WORD ADDICTIVE, WHICH CAN SOMETIMES ALSO BE TRUE. ADDITIVES IN FOOD AND DRINK ARE USUALLY PUT THERE FOR APPEAL FACTOR. THINGS ARE MADE SWEETER, BRIGHTER, OR A COMPLETELY DIFFERENT COLOUR SO THAT YOU, THE CONSUMER, ARE MORE LIKELY TO PURCHASE IT. FORTUNATELY, WE ARE NOW STARTING TO LEARN OF THE NEGATIVE & ADDICTIVE PROPERTIES OF SOME, AND CAN MAKE BETTER & MORE EDUCATED CHOICES FOR YOU AND YOUR LOVED ONES.

PRESERVATIVES

PRESERVATIVES ARE ADDED TO OUR FOOD AND DRINKS TO EXTEND SHELF LIFE. (THE AMOUNT OF TIME IT TAKES FOR A PRODUCT TO GO "BAD") MANY OF OUR FAVOURITE FOODS ARE ONLY AVAILABLE TO US BECAUSE OF A FORM OF PRESERVATION. THE HEALTHIEST OPTIONS ARE PICKLED, JAMMED, AND FROZEN, BUT BEWARE.. A LOT OF SHELVED FOOD/DRINK ARE PRESERVED WITH ARTIFICIAL CHEMICALS.

HOW TO READ A LABEL

LOOK HERE FIRST
THE SERVING SIZE SHOULD BE THE FIRST THING YOU LOOK AT AS ALL OTHER VALUES DEPEND ON THE AMOUNT OF SERVINGS YOU ARE CONSUMING. THE DAILY VALUES LISTED IN THE NUTRITIONAL FACTS ARE NOT NECESSARILY FOR THE AMOUNT YOU HAVE IN YOUR HAND OR ON YOUR PLATE..

THE "% DV" (% OF DAILY VALUE) IS BASED OFF OF THE RDA (RECOMMENDED DIETARY ALLOWANCE) FOR THE AVERAGE ADULT - BASED OFF OF AVERAGE METABOLISM, AND THE AVERAGE BODY'S NEEDS, SO KEEP IN MIND, A GROWING PERSON (YOU) WOULD HAVE DIFFERENT DAILY NEEDS THAN A GROWN ADULT CONSUMING 2000 CALORIES A DAY.

NUTRITIONAL FACTS
8 servings per container
Serving size.   2/3 cup (55g)

Amount per one serving
Calories 230

% DV*		
12%	**Total Fat** 8g	
5%	Saturated Fat 1g	
	Trans Fat 0g	
0%	**Cholesterol** 0mg	
7%	**Sodium** 160mg	
12%	**Total Carbs** 37g	
14%	Dietary Fibre 4g	
	Sugars 1g	
	Added Sugars 0g	
	Protein 3g	
10%	**Vitamin D** 2 mcg	
20%	**Calcium** 250 mg	
45%	**Iron** 8 mg	
5%	**Potassium** 235 mg	

INGREDIENTS:

NUTRITIONAL VALUES
ALONG WITH A % AMOUNT, THERE WILL ALSO BE A MEASUREMENT AMOUNT. THIS WILL USUALLY BE IN GRAMS (g), OR MILLIGRAMS (mg), BUT CAN SOMETIMES EVEN BE AS SMALL AS MICROGRAMS (mcg)! THIS NUMBER IS THE BEST VALUE TO LOOK AT WHEN MAKING YOUR NUTRITIONAL CHOICES BECAUSE, UNLIKE THE % VALUE, IS NOT A NUMBER BASED ON THE "AVERAGE ADULT'S" NEEDS. NOT ONLY DO YOU NEED EXTRA NUTRIENTS TO FUEL YOUR SUPER SPEED GROWTH, BUT..
YOU ARE SO MUCH GREATER THAN AVERAGE!

INGREDIENTS
THIS SECTION CAN OFTEN BE THE MOST RESOURCEFUL, AS IT GIVES YOU THE ABILITY TO LEARN IF YOUR NUTRIENTS ARE COMING FROM TRUE, WHOLE SOURCES, OR ARTIFICIAL ONES. IT GIVES YOU INSIGHT TO LEARN ABOUT YOUR INTOLERANCES, AND ALSO THE FOODS YOUR BODY RESPONDS WELL TO. IN MOST COUNTRIES, INGREDIENTS ARE LEGALLY REQUIRED TO BE LISTED IN QUANTITY ORDER, SO THE FIRST INGREDIENT YOU SEE WILL BE THE ONE THERE IS MOST OF.

RULE OF THUMB
TRY TO NOT CONSUME FOOD WITH INGREDIENTS THAT YOU CAN'T PRONOUNCE, UNLESS YOU'VE DONE RESEARCH FIRST..

FOOD GROUPS

'Traditional' food groups were created by health and governing authorities, and are part of a simplified guide for recommended daily food intake and physical activity. These guides have historically provided 4 major food groups, (Fruits & Vegetables, Grains or Starchy Carbohydrates, Meat & alternatives, and Milk & alternatives) and gives recommendations such as number of servings and serving sizes. Each country has it's own 'Food Guide', but most began, and remain, somewhat comparable. Recent studies from independent sources, like The Heart Foundation and Universities, that show a more optimal way of eating, have been mirrored with many countries updating their recommendations, while others remain 'traditional'; this can often be for cultural or socioeconomic reasons, or due to the lack of local research or access. Some of the biggest changes are the recognition of whole wheat and fruits & vegetables in optimal health, and in the connections between red meat (steak etc) & risk of cardiovascular issues.

VEGETABLES AND FRUIT

Choose Fruits & Veggies that are:
- Colourful
- High in Variety
- Without Added Sugar

Should be 50% of plate
see page 52 for more.

GRAIN PRODUCTS

Choose WHOLE Grain foods such as
- Quinoa
- Wild Rice
- Whole Grain Pasta

Should be 25% of plate
see page 51 for more.

PROTEIN PRODUCTS

Choose Protein Sources that are:
- Primarily Plant Based
- Lean & Low Sodium

Should be 25% of plate
see page 55 for more.

Canada (2020)
- 50% fruit & veggies
- 25% Protein
- 25% Grains
- +WATER

Australia (2013)
- 44% fruit & veggies
- 12.5% Dairy
- 12.5% Protein
- 31% Carbs
- +WATER

USA (2016)
- 50% fruit & veggies
- 25% Protein
- 25% Grains
- +3 cups MILK

U.K. (2016)
- 40% fruit & veggies
- 8% Dairy
- 12% Protein
- 1% Oils
- 38% Carbs
- +WATER

GRAINS

A GRAIN IS..

"..a small, hard, dry seed, with or without an attached hull or fruit layer, harvested for human or animal consumption." A <u>grain crop</u> is a grain-producing plant.

GRAIN CULTIVATION

The two main types of commercial grain crops are cereals and legumes. After being harvested, dry grains are more durable than other staple foods, which makes them well suited to industrial agriculture, since they can be mechanically harvested, transported by rail or ship, stored for long periods in silos, milled for flour and pressed for oil. Major global markets exist for maize, rice, soybeans, wheat and other grains. The development of grain agriculture allowed excess food to be produced and stored easily which may have led to the creation of the first permanent settlements & the division of society into classes." See Pg. 74 & 121

WHOLE GRAIN VS REFINED

'Whole Grain' means that the grain kernel is intact, or whole. It contains all THREE layers - Bran, Germ, and Endosperm - each with their own nutritional benefits. 'Refined Grains' are MILLED, which makes a fine powder, with a longer 'shelf life'. This removes both the Bran AND Germ layers, which reduces Dietary Fibre, Magnesium, Iron, and other Vitamins & Minerals.

TYPES OF GRAIN

QUINOA
Gluten-free
High in Protein
Contains all essential AA's
High in Dietary Fibre

WILD RICE
High in antioxidants
Good Nutrient Proportions
Anti-inflammatory
Helps with cholesterol control

OATS
High Nutrient Density
Low Sodium
High in Good Fats
Very Good for Digestion

LOOK FOR THE WHOLE GRAIN STAMPS
LIKE CANADA'S!

PSSST.. A DIET <u>HIGH</u> IN WHOLE GRAINS SHOWS REDUCED HEART DISEASE VS. A DIET WITH <u>LOW</u> WHOLE GRAIN CONSUMPTION.

FRUITS

A FRUIT IS..

..a seed-bearing structure that develops from the ovary of a flowering plant.

FRUIT CULTIVATION

"POMOLOGY (FROM LATIN POMUM, "FRUIT") STUDIES FRUIT AND ITS CULTIVATION. ONE INVOLVED IN THE SCIENCE OF POMOLOGY IS CALLED A POMOLOGIST."

Just like the colourful flowers you see in gardens, a fruit will only fully form if the plant is healthy, strong, and in the right environment to thrive. Therefore, fruit is (typically) less hardy than vegetables, and more prone to environmental limitations. (See Page 115)

BIG BENEFITS:

- Natural Sugars for Energy
- High Nutrient Density
- Fruit makes GREAT snacks
- Experience flavours from all over the world
- Fun & beautiful colours
- Yummy ways to get lots of nutrients
- Major export (pg. 74)

APPLES
One contains approx.
4.4g of fibre
8.4mg of Vitamin C
Helps keep your heart strong

LEMONS
One contains approx.
15mg of Calcium
30mg of Vitamin C
Helps with Iron absorption

BANANA
One contains approx.
23g of Carbohydrates
358mg of Potassium
Natural Mood Booster

PINEAPPLE
One cup contains approx.
2.6mg of Manganese
79mg of Vitamin C
Natural anti-inflammatory

BLUEBERRY
One cup contains approx.
4g of fibre
15g of Carbohydrates
84% Water
Low Calorie
Good source of:
Vit K, Vit C, and Manganese
VERY high source of:
anti-oxidants (pg. 88)

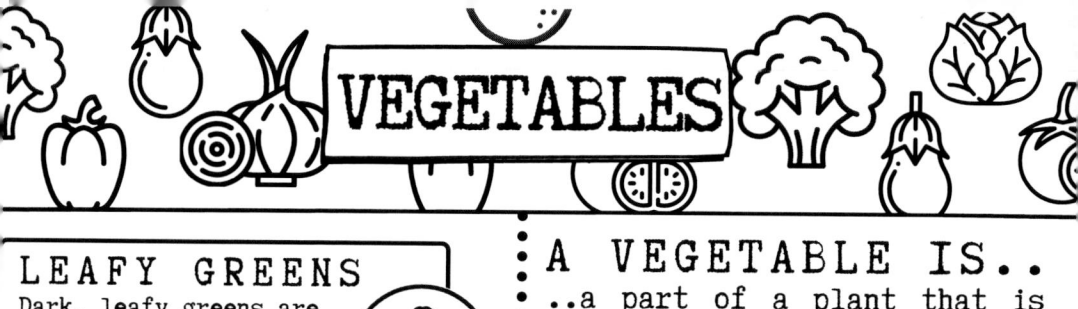

VEGETABLES

LEAFY GREENS
Dark, leafy greens are SUPER rich in vitamins, minerals, AND fibre!
Try.. Microgreens · Kale · Spinach · Collard Greens · Arugula · Romaine

ROOT VEGGIES
Root veggies are usually heavier and flavourful, and come in a range of colours, each with it's unique nutrient blend.
Try.. Beet · Parsnip · Radish · Ginger · Turnip ·

RAINBOW POWER
Pssst.. want to know the secret to tapping into all the POWER of veggies?

FILL YOUR PLATE WITH AS MANY COLOURS AS YOU CAN!

- See page 95 -

BROCCOLI
- High in Vit K
- More Vit C than Oranges!
- Good source of Protein & Fibre
- Potent Antioxidants

No Wonder it's a "SUPERFOOD!"

A VEGETABLE IS..
..a part of a plant that is consumed by humans or other animals as food; typically the roots, leaves, or stems.

TIMING OF HARVEST
Every living thing, including plants, has a life cycle; so, as a plant grows, so does it's nutrient content, but, as a plant dies, it's nutrients do too. Ideally, we would harvest at peak ripeness and immediately before consumption, however, this is rarely the case. Most of our fruits & veggies come from far away, and there is a long journey to get to the store, and then to your home, so many are picked long before ripeness so they won't rot. One of the best options for nutrient security of non-local sources, is "flash frozen" produce, as those are picked ripe and immediately frozen, which secures maximum nutrients until consumption.

BIG BENEFITS:
Most can be eaten in abundance
Many can be cultivated at home
Great source of most nutrients
Usually low in calories

..PLUS SOME OF THE MOST NUTRIENT-DENSE FOODS ARE VEGGIES!!

Meat has been a major food source for as long as humans have been in the food chain! If you've been to a museum, or studied the cavemen at school, you've probably already seen the weapons and tactics that were used to hunt animals, not just for food, but also for fur for warmth. We have come to expect meat as part of our meals still, and not having it can sometimes leave you feeling unfulfilled. Meat is also a very important part of culture for many people around the world, and can be a wonderful way to expose yourself to flavours and ways of different lands and life.

Whether it's a farm, a factory or otherwise, meat production provides work and income to countless families, and even entire communities. However, with advancing technology and larger corporations wanting to take on that human demand, smaller farms are finding themselves competing with a new form of meat product: that of mass production. While larger meat producers are able to offer you their meat products at a lower price, that reduction is because of costs cut within production. This could be replacing people with machines, lower quality feed for animals, or a number of other ethical and environmental issues that lead to both moral dilemmas and nutrient deficient meat. This is just ONE reason to support local. (Page 56 & 108)

MYTHBUSTER

Meat has long been known as our major source of protein, and is often wrongly believed to be our only source, and therefore needed for survival. This is far from the truth, and while meat is a nutrient source, it is generally has LESS nutrient value than plants, and has been proven to not be essential for survival. Below are some examples of plant sources of protein for comparison.. (per 100g)

Chicken: 31g   Beef: 26g   Soy beans: 36g
Chickpeas: 19g   Lentils: 26g   Hemp Seeds: 33g

COWS IN THE FOOD INDUSTRY

Although beef is not the world's most consumed meat, cows are also used for their milk products, making them one of the largest populations of livestock. In countries like Brazil, Australia & USA, where "cattle" is a lifeline, there is a due, and almost patriotic, pride to be taken in the culture of raising cattle as such.

SYMBIOTIC
"..to be in a mutually beneficial relationship with another person/group"

When it comes to cows (& chickens too!), humans have created a now symbiotic relationship in which we get food, and (when treated right) the cows are able to live well with ample access to good quality food, shelter, warmth & protection from other predators.

THINGS TO THINK ABOUT

MASS PRODUCTION
MASS PRODUCTION IN ANY FORM IS NEVER USUALLY A GOOD THING, BUT MASS PRODUCTION FOR ANIMALS USUALLY ENTAILS BRUTAL AND INHUMANE TREATMENT.

FEED
NUTRITION MATTERS JUST AS MUCH TO OUR FOOD'S FOOD AS IT DOES TO US. HIGHER QUALITY FEED MEANS HIGHER QUALITY FOOD.

WHAT CAN YOU DO?
IF YOU DO CONSUME COW PRODUCTS, WHETHER IT IS BEEF OR BYPRODUCTS LIKE MILK AND CHEESE, THE SINGLE MOST IMPORTANT THING IS TO ENSURE QUALITY; WHICH IN TURN MEANS ENSURING THE TREATMENT OF THE ANIMALS IS HUMANE AND ETHICAL; IN MOST CASES, THE BEST WAY TO DO THIS IS:

SUPPORT LOCAL FARMERS

DID YOU KNOW?
Reducing your "red meat" intake can greatly reduce your risk of heart health issues...

...what is...
'ORGANIC'

ORGANIC is a certification that says the production of a food was without the use of chemicals or other artificial agents, including fertilizer & pesticides. The list of banned substances aims to protect consumers from potentially dangerous, and often unknown, effects of these chemicals.

WHAT IT TAKES

THE PURPOSE OF THE CERTIFICATION IS TO BE ABLE TO OFFER THE CONSUMER (YOU) THE CLOSEST THING TO A GUARANTEE. TO MAKE SURE THIS IS POSSIBLE, BECOMING CERTIFIED IS NOT EASY, AND INCLUDE RULES & REGULATIONS THAT GO BACK A NUMBER OF YEARS; INCLUDING THAT LAND BE A MINUMUM DISTANCE FROM EXPOSURE TO CHEMICALS. WHILST THIS IS THE REASON WE CAN DEPEND ON THE CERTIFICATION, IT CAN MAKE IT DIFFICULT FOR NEW OR SMALLER FARMS TO GET CERT- IFIED. CAN YOU IMAGINE..? YOU PURCHASE YOUR IST FARM, INVEST EVERYTHING TO OFFER CLEAN, WHOLE CROP & NEVER USE ANY CHEMICALS.. BUT.. HAVE A NEIGHBOUR THAT DOES? YOU MAY NOT GET CERTIFIED.

WHO CERTIFIES?

ORGANIC CERTIFICATION IS NOT A GLOBAL PROGRAM, BUT RATHER A COLLECTION OF PROGRAMS AROUND THE WORLD. THIS MEANS THAT THE CERTIFICATE IS ISSUED BY A DIFFERENT PLACE DEPENDING ON THE COUNTRY IN WHICH YOU ARE APPLYING, BUT THAT THE GENERAL RULES AND STANDARDS ARE VERY SIMILAR GLOBALLY. EACH COUNTRY WILL HAVE A SEAL OR LOGO THAT HELPS YOU FIND ORGANICALLY CERTIFIED PRODUCTS...

THIS IS CANADA'S

ALTERNATIVE HEALTHY OPTIONS

GRASS-FED

GRASS-FED USUALLY REFERS TO CATTLE, AND CAN BE FOUND ON THINGS LIKE STEAK & BURGERS. GRASS-FED LIVESTOCK ARE TYPICALLY HEALTHIER ANIMALS.

FREE RANGE

FREE RANGE IS USUALLY FOUND IN FARM BIRDS LIKE CHICKEN, AND MEANS THAT THE ANIMALS WERE FREE TO ROAM AND FORAGE THE LAND. STUDIES SHOW THIS MAKES FOR CLEANER MEAT.

TRY TO AVOID:
- INGREDIENTS YOU CANNOT PRONOUNCE
- BASING FOOD DECISIONS ON ORGANIC CERTIFICATION ALONE

TRY TO SUPPORT LOCAL

MEALS

Having nutrient-dense, well-timed meals, is VITAL to optimal daily functioning. Your brain needs constant and efficient fuel to stay focused, your muscles need enough for sports and recovery, and your growth and mood needs you to have balance and variety to continue running the way it should for you to thrive.

BREAKFAST

Breakfast is the kickstarter for your body and mind each morning, which is why it is often called the most important meal! It fires up your metabolism, digestion and alertness.

LUNCH

Lunch is your needed refuel. By this time, your body has cycled through much of your breakfast energy, and, if you skipped a mid morning snack, you are probably pretty hungry by now!

DINNER

Due to our daily demands, like work, school and sports, dinner has become that one time in the day where (if you're lucky) you get to sit down with your family and bond. Dinner is important for so many reasons, but it is the best for your digestion to try not to eat within 2 hours of bedtime.

DESSERTS

Ooh, desserts! Raise your hand if this is your favourite meal, & keep it up if it's the only meal you feel "bad" about. Well, get ready, because it does not have to be that way!! 'Desserts' have a reputation to be full of "bad" ingredients, and some of your favourites likely are, but we are discovering DELICIOUS alternatives to these all the time! Try researching the ingredients of your favourites to see if you can trade any for a more natural & nutritious option, or visit www.kedounion.com for recipes, tips and challenges.

SNACKS

Think of snacks like.. power ups; the right snack can increase your speed, power, mind and mood! Snacks should be spaced between meals, but, having a snack on hand, just in case, can save you from falling asleep on your desk and help you maintain a positive and patient mood through the day! See below for some good ideas.

SNACK IDEAS

- HomeMade Power Bars (Page 104)
- HomeMade Fruit & Nut Mix
- Veggies & Hummus or Peanut Butter
- HomeMade Healthy "Desserts"
- Pineapple, Banana, or Watermelon
- Vegetable or Fruit Chips (Page 106)
- A Smoothie (if you can)

DIETS

MEAT ↑ ↓ PLANTS

CARNIVORE
MEAT ONLY
- most wilds cats

OMNIVORE
MEAT & VEGETATION MIX
- most humans are omnivores

PALEO
HUNTER/GATHERER
- usually no grain or dairy

PESCATARIAN
NO MEAT
- no animal flesh, except fish

PLANT BASED
PLANTS ONLY
- including vegetarian & vegan

RAW
NO HEAT
- usually plant-based

These are only a few of the many diets out there based on preference, restrictions and limitation

WHAT DECIDES A DIET

WHAT YOUR DIET CONSISTS OF IS OFTEN NOT UP TO CHOICE. NATURE CAN PLAY A HUGE ROLE IN YOUR DIETARY LIMITATIONS. SOME OF THE MAJOR FACTORS ARE:

AVAILABILITY & COST
As you'll later see, or may already know, many foods can only be cultivated in certain environments, and it is a luxury for us to be able to enjoy them! As availability decreases, cost rises.

MEDICAL LIMITATIONS
This includes allergies and intolerances, but there are also many other medical conditions that can affect your diet.. like diabetes, IBS, organ malfunctions, anemia, or a hyper thyroid.

NATURE VS NURTURE

IN THIS CASE, NURTURE REFERS TO CHOICE, WHETHER IT BE YOURS OR YOUR CAREGIVERS'. THE CHOICE FOR YOUR DIET CAN USUALLY BE DUE TO ONE OF THESE MAJOR FACTORS:

- **MORALITY**
  ie. no meat

- **RELIGION**
  ie. no pig products

- **CULTURAL**
  ie. self cultivators

- **TASTEBUDS**
  ie. squid is yucky!

WHAT "DIET" IS RIGHT FOR ME

RULE #1- LISTEN TO YOUR CAREGIVERS

THIS IS ONE OF THOSE SITUATIONS WHERE, AT LEAST WHILE YOU ARE GROWING, YOUR PARENTS KNOW BEST. THEY HAVE MONITERED AND PROVIDED YOUR NUTRITION SINCE BEFORE YOU WERE BORN, AND UNTIL YOU LEARN TO ADVOCATE FOR YOURSELF, YOUR PARENTS ARE YOUR ADVOCATES.

RULE #2- EXPLORE WITH FOOD

UNLESS UNDER YOUR PARENTS OR A DOCTOR'S GUIDANCE, OR YOU HAVE ALLERGIES/INTOLERANCES, YOU SHOULD NEVER TRY TO RESTRICT YOURSELF FROM CERTAIN FOODS OR ORIGINS. AS YOU'LL LATER READ, EXPOSURE TO CULTURES AND FLAVOURS IS SOUL FOOD AS WELL.. FIND OUT WHAT YOU LIKE, WHAT YOU <u>THRIVE</u> ON, AND REMEMBER, YOUR TASTEBUDS DON'T STOP CHANGING, NEITHER SHOULD YOU.

RULE #3- LEARN YOUR INTOLERANCES

WORK WITH YOUR CAREGIVERS OR A PROFESSIONAL TO LEARN ABOUT YOUR ALLERGIES, INTOLERANCES OR POTENTIAL MEDICAL ISSUES THAT COULD AFFECT YOUR NUTRITION. YOUR PARENTS HAVE LIKELY EXPOSED YOU TO A LOT ALREADY, BUT OTHERS MAY BE GENETIC, AND COULD AFFECT YOU LATER ON. WHILE YOU ARE YOUNG AND GROWING, YOUR NUTRITION CAN HELP BUILD THE RIGHT FOUNDATION FOR LONG TERM HEALTH, RESILIENCE & HAPPINESS.

secret recipe

Homemade Burgers (Omnivore)

SERVES: 8
TIME: 30

DIRECTIONS

1. In a large mixing bowl, combine Beef, Garlic, Onion, Black Pepper & Seasoning Salt. Mix by hand until well combined and until no clumps of meat remain.

2. Add in Worcestershire, BBQ, Ketchup, and Egg. Mix until well combined. Most effective by hand, but use masher if preferred!

3. Finally add Breadcrumbs, Almond Meal or alternative. Thsi should bring your mixture to a thicker consistency that is easily formed into 8 patties. Your mixture should not be too liquid-y but also not crumbly or dry. You can add in a splash of water, 1 egg, or a little oil, or more breadcrumbs if needed.

4. Heat non-stick frying pan with Oil over medium heat.

5. Fry burger patties for a few minutes on each side, until fully cooked through, & serve!!

------- YOU'LL NEED --------

- Mixing Bowl
- Frying Pan
- Spatula
- Burger Fixin's!

INGREDIENTS

- 2 lbs Lean Ground Beef
- 1 Large Egg
- 2 tsp Black Pepper
- 2 tsp Seasoning Salt
- 1/4 cup Breadcrumbs or Almond Meal (or alt.)
- 1/8 cup Tomato Ketchup
- 1/8 cup BBQ Sauce
- 3 tbs Worcestershire Sauce
- 2 cloves minced Garlic
- 1/8 cup minced Red Onion

NUTRITIONAL INFO
PER ONE SERVING

Calories 226
Total Fat 10.7g
   Saturated 4.7g
   Trans 0.5g
   Polyunsat 0.0g
   Monounsat 0.0g
Cholesterol 70mg
Sodium 315.2mg
Total Carbs 9.2g
   Dietary Fibre . 0.9g
   Sugar 4.1g
   Added Sugars . 0g
Protein 24.4g
Vitamin D 0%
Calcium 15.9%
Iron 17.6%
Potassium 120.9mg
Vitamin A 2.3%
Vitamin C 3.4

secret recipe

Veggie Burgers (Plant Based)

SERVES: 8
TIME: 55

DIRECTIONS

1. Preheat oven to 400F and line baking sheet with parchment paper.

2. Roast Sweet Potato on baking sheet for 30-40 mins or until slightly soft, & set aside.

3. Combine Quinoa & Water in small saucepan. Bring to a boil, then reduce to simmer until all water is absorbed. Remove from heat, cover & let sit for 10 mins.

4. Combine cooled sweet potatoes, quinoa, black beans, onion, cilantro, garlic, paprika, cumin, salt, pepper & hemp seeds in a bowl, and mix until well combined (a potato masher works well!).

5. Add in Oats and hand-mix.

6. Shape your mixture into 8 patties (approx 1.2 cup each)

7. Heat non-stick frying pan with Oil over medium heat.

8. Fry burger patties for a few minutes on each side, until golden and crispy & serve!!

-------- YOU'LL NEED --------

- Oven
- Mixing Bowl
- Potato Masher
- Baking Sheet
- Saucepan
- Frying Pan & Spatula
- Burger Fixin's

INGREDIENTS

- 1 1/2 lbs Sweet Potato
- 1/2 cup Quinoa (rinsed)
- 1 cup Water
- 1 can (15oz) Black Beans (rinsed & drained)
- 1/2 cup chopped Red Onion
- 1/3 cup chopped Cilantro
- 2 cloves Pressed Garlic
- 2 tsp Smoked Paprika
- 2 tsp Ground Cumin
- 1 tsp Chili Powder
- 1/4 tsp Black Pepper
- 1/2 tsp Pink Sea Salt
- 1 cup fine blended Oats
- 4 tbs Hemp Seeds

NUTRITIONAL INFO
PER ONE SERVING

- Calories 240
- Total Fat 4.6g
  - Saturated 0.5g
  - Trans 0g
  - Polyunsat 2.8g
  - Monounsat 0.8g
- Cholesterol 0mg
- Sodium 159.7mg
- Total Carbs 40.9g
  - Dietary Fibre . 8.6g
  - Sugar 4.9g
  - Added Sugars . 0g
- Protein 9.5g
- Vitamin D 0%
- Calcium 16.8%
- Iron 15.9%
- Potassium 584.1mg
- Vitamin A 262.5%
- Vitamin C 9.5

secret recipe

Fish Burgers (Pescatarian)

SERVES: 4
TIME: 15

DIRECTIONS

1. In a mixing bowl, flake apart salmon (be careful not to overmash)

2. Add all remaining ingredients into bowl by hand. Your mixture should have a consistency thick enough to form into 4 medium patties. Add a little oil (or splash of water), or extra Almond Meal (or alternative) to change consistency.

3. Heat non-stick frying pan with Avocado Oil over medium heat.

4. Fry burger patties for a few minutes on each side, until golden and crispy.

5. Place patties on paper towel & sprinkle with a little extra Pink Salt or Lemon Juice for added POW.

6. Serve on a fresh bun with all your favourite fixin's!!

------- YOU'LL NEED --------
- Frying Pan
- Spatula
- Mixing Bowl
- Paper Towel
- Burger Fixin's!

INGREDIENTS
- 12-14 oz Cooked/Canned Atlantic Salmon
- 1/2 cup Almond Meal
- 2 Eggs
- 1 tsp Himalayan Pink Salt
- 1 tsp Black Pepper
- 1/2 tsp Garlic Powder
- 1/8 cup Fresh Parsley
- 1/8 cup Fresh Dill
- 3 tbs Lemon Juice
- 1 tsp Avocado Oil
- + extra for frying pan

NUTRITIONAL INFO
PER ONE SERVING
- Calories 223
- Total Fat 15.8g
  - Saturated 3.2g
  - Trans 0g
  - Polyunsat 1.4g
  - Monounsat 4.4g
- Cholesterol 124.9mg
- Sodium 491.9mg
- Total Carbs 2.3g
  - Dietary Fibre . 0.8g
  - Sugar 0.4g
  - Added Sugars . 0g
- Protein 16.5g
- Vitamin D 0%
- Calcium 22%
- Iron 2.3%
- Potassium 84.2mg
- Vitamin A 47.1%
- Vitamin C 8.6

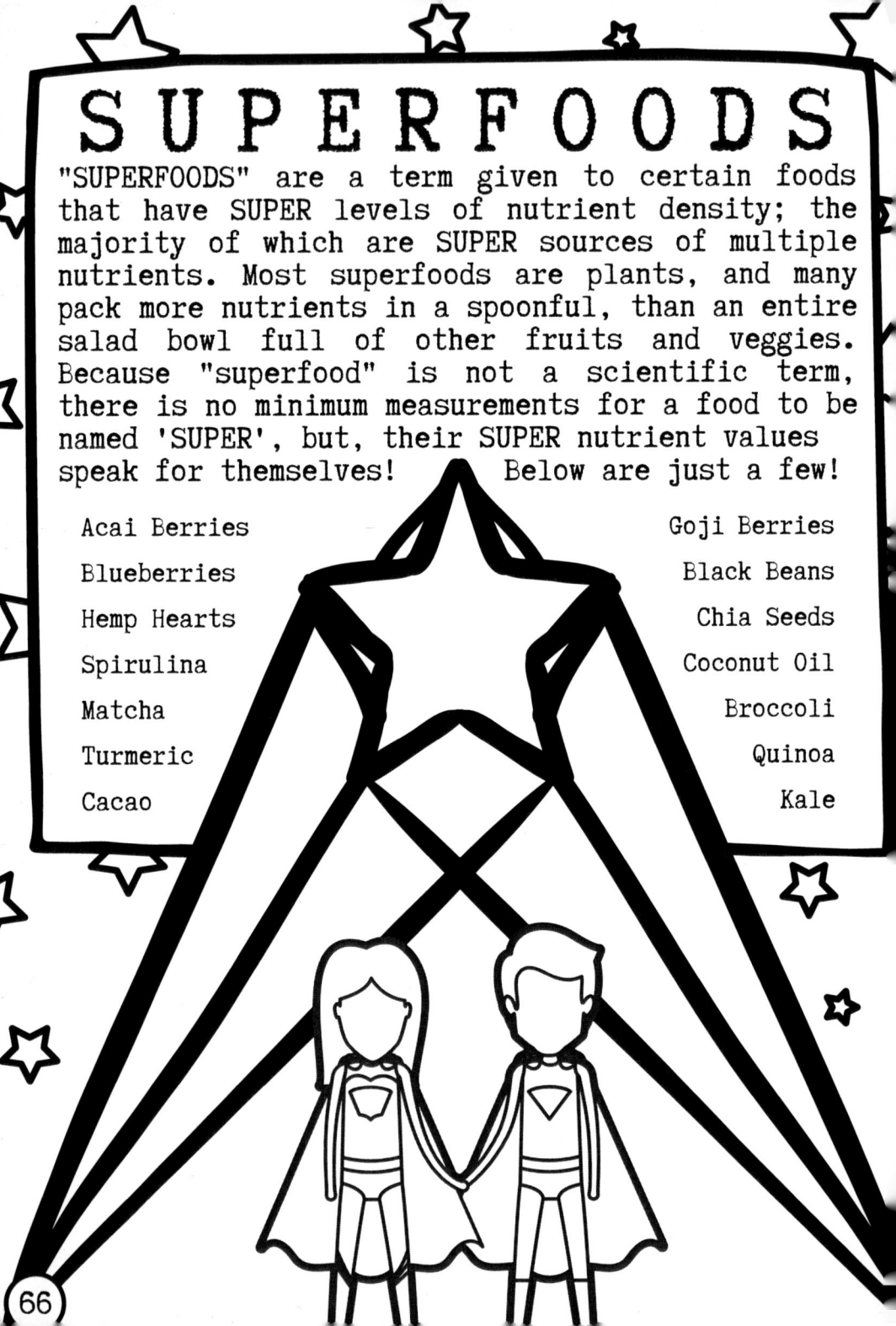

SUPERFOODS

"SUPERFOODS" are a term given to certain foods that have SUPER levels of nutrient density; the majority of which are SUPER sources of multiple nutrients. Most superfoods are plants, and many pack more nutrients in a spoonful, than an entire salad bowl full of other fruits and veggies. Because "superfood" is not a scientific term, there is no minimum measurements for a food to be named 'SUPER', but, their SUPER nutrient values speak for themselves! Below are just a few!

- Acai Berries
- Blueberries
- Hemp Hearts
- Spirulina
- Matcha
- Turmeric
- Cacao

- Goji Berries
- Black Beans
- Chia Seeds
- Coconut Oil
- Broccoli
- Quinoa
- Kale

EARTH'S BIOMES & ECOSYSTEMS

Our beautiful planet is filled with as much diversity in it's environments & ecosystems as it has in it's animal populations. From snow to sun and sand to rock, we can find forms of life; with some climates offering the ability to THRIVE more than others. Earth's BIOMES each have beautiful and defining individuality, from it's climate to it's inhabitants and resources for life. See if you can find all of the biome related words below!

```
A Y H F C R A I N F O R E S T O L J E
D E T T G L O F A T L N H A E R E X B
T B G I L A T R Y E D K B V J D S T E
U O P Y U T O L R S U S T A I N O O C
N Y R F H F K S B T J E Q N E T R A O
D M L U T R O P I C A L D N Q G X O S
R H I R A E O D D N U G X A J F A I Y
A H E G I S G H N A S U L D M P F R S
S H L X G H U A F E B G L T A O S M T
L U N F A W V I P O D I T O R E R S E
G L P O K A N A D L N N O X I T L O M
F O R E S T L T I C Y W M M N J H I L
B F R D L E E N V I R O N M E N T E X
L Y S F M R I O N B Y H S N A B O V Z
D S E T R V Q P W R E S O U R C E S M
O M O U N T A I N I C T B O H M S C A
A I L S C J L T E M P E R A T E Y R D
```

Tropical	Rainforest	Savanna
Taiga	Tundra	Mountain
Temperate	Forest	Marine
Biome	Freshwater	Environment
Ecosystem	Sustain	Resources

around the world

FOOD

FOOD SECURITY

"A SITUATION THAT EXISTS WHEN ALL PEOPLE, AT ALL TIMES, HAVE PHYSICAL, SOCIAL & ECONOMICAL ACCESS TO SUFFICIENT, SAFE AND NUTRITIOUS FOOD THAT MEETS THEIR DIETARY NEEDS AND FOOD PREFERENCES FOR AN ACTIVE AND HEALTHY LIFE."

TO ACHIEVE THIS, FOOD MUST BE THE FOLLOWING:

'4A FRAMEWORK'

AVAILABLE   ACCESSIBLE

ACCEPTABLE   ADEQUATE

THE REALITY

DESPITE FOOD SECURITY HAVING BEEN DECLARED A BASIC HUMAN RIGHT (AS PER THE 'UNIVERSAL DECLARATION OF HUMAN RIGHTS', ADOPTED BY THE UN GENERAL ASSEMBLY IN 1948, 1966), MORE THAN A QUARTER OF THE GLOBAL POPULATION LIVES WITH MODERATE TO SEVERE FOOD INSECURITY. DESPITE THERE BEING ENOUGH FOOD PRODUCTION TO FEED THE GLOBAL POPULATION, A SEVERE DISTRIBUTION IMBALANCE LEAVES SOME WITH TOO MUCH, AND MANY WITH TOO LITTLE; BOTH FORMS OF MALNOURISHMENT. UNDERSTANDING THIS GAP WILL REQUIRE A GLOBAL VIEW ON SOCIO-ECONOMIC STATUS AND SUSTAINABILITY.

CULTURE

FOR THE LOVE OF FOOD

FOOD IS RESPONSIBLE FOR SO MUCH OF THE HUMAN POPULATIONS' SOCIETAL BUILD; WHETHER BY WAY OF CULTIVATION, PREPARATION, TRADITION OR CULTURE. BIRTHDAY CAKE, WEDDING CAKE, THANKSGIVING TURKEY AND GRANDMA'S SECRET RECIPES ARE JUST SOME OF THE MORE GLOBALLY RECOGNIZED FOOD TRADITIONS, BUT THESE ARE JUST GLIMPSES INTO THE DEPTHS OF THE CULTURE FOOD & NUTRITION HOLD AROUND THE WORLD. NOT ONLY DO THEY BRING US TOGETHER ON A PERSONAL LEVEL, BUT FOOD HAS BEEN USED AS A MEANS TO BOAST LAND, IT'S PEOPLE, SKILLS, RICHES AND TO GAIN SOCIOECONOMIC STATUS & SOURCES OF COMMUNITY REVENUE. (SEE PAGE 74)

WORLDLY CUISINES

BELOW WE HAVE LISTED JUST A FEW OF THE WORLD'S MOST DELICIOUS CUISINES. SEE IF YOU CAN FIND THEIR ORIGINS & ENLIGHTEN YOURSELF WITH ANY MEANING/HISTORY.

Jerk Chicken	Spaghetti	Wonton
_____	_____	_____
Sushi	Crepes	Enchilada
_____	_____	_____
Pad Krapow Gai	Kolokythokeftedes	
_____	_____	

Malnutrition, or malnourishment, comes in many forms and, although you probably imagine an underweight, sick person, malnutrition refers to imbalances of a person's intake of energy and/or nutrients, including both deficiency AND excess.

- Undernourished
- Micronutrient-related malnutrition
- Overweight, obese & diet-related diseases

STAGES OF MALNOURISHMENT

NOTE: Physical signs and symptoms are the last stage of malnourishment, which means a lot of damage has already been done by the time it may be noticed. This is why getting to know your body and your food is so important.

| INADEQUATE INTAKE | DECREASED STORES & TISSUE LEVELS | ALTERED BIOCHEMICAL & PHYSIOLOGICAL FUNCTIONS | PHYSICAL SIGNS & SYMPTOMS |

MALNOURISHMENT VERSUS OBESITY

Obesity is known as a double edged sword, as both the imbalance of nutrients, and the stress of excess fat on the body, both have sets of health concerns. Addressing obesity is a longer, slower process and should never be unduly rushed; but it requires a deficit in energy (or calories). On the nutritional side, an imbalance will have had negative effects on both your body and mind, but requires much more immediate resolution. Treatment of malnourishment in any form must be at the direction of a professional.

MYTHBUSTER

OBESE = "FAT" = "over nourished"

WORLD HUNGER

The cycle of world hunger and it's consequences is a life long battle starting in-utero, passing from parent to child with snowballing effects. Worldwide, and especially in those living in hunger & without food security, face prominent and recorded deficiencies in Energy, Iron (60-80% of world population), Iodine (3-30%), Folate (26%), Protein (12%), Calcium (50%) and others; increasing the risk of neural tube defects, infant mortality, anemia, developmental retardation, stunting, infection, blindness, weakness, lethargy, compromised reproductive & immune systems, and osteoporosis (among countless others). When you think of world hunger, your mind likely goes to somewhat unrelateable, perhaps almost other-worldly, images of those affected; but food insecurity, malnourishment & hunger affects people on a global scale. In fact, you likely know many already, as unfortunately, it is all around us. (See Page 76)

WORLD FACTS
- There is enough food in the world to feed entire population adequately
- World hunger can be cured with $7-265b USD
- 6.9 million people live with severe food insecurity (8.9%)
- Rate of stunting: 21.3%
- 122 million children affected by stunting live in 'high conflict'
- Vit A deficiency is leading cause of blindness in children

MOST AT RISK
- Those in poverty
- Single mothers under 25 years old
- Minority communities
- Indigenous communities
- Off-reserve Indigenous person(s)
- Civil unrest victims
- Abuse victims
- Pregnant women
- Remote locations
  - specifically children & infants

ORGANIZATIONS THAT HELP
Bread for the World Institute www.bread.org
CARE www.care.org
Free from Hunger www.freefromhunger.org
World Food Programme www.wfp.org
Oxfam Canada www.oxfam.ca
The United Nations Children's Fund (UNICEF) www.unicef.org
World Health Organization (WHO) www.who.int
The International Fund for Agricultural Development (IFAD) www.ifad.org

resources & access

UNDERSTANDING THE ISSUES

There are endless factors that contribute to the range of hunger, thirst, obesity & health statistics around the world. Below, we have listed some of the most common limitations, but above all, having both the RESOURCES and ACCESS TO THEM is prevalent as the world's biggest inhibitor to food and water needs. Over your lifetime, you WILL face a form of limitation in one way or another, but never lose sight of the fact it is a blessing to make it past #I on the list; many are currently not so lucky, and need our help.

FOOD LIMITATIONS

1. Geography, income, physical limitations, allergies
2. Social Acceptance (upbringing, peers)
3. Personal Acceptance (religion, background)
4. Psych & Emotional (comfort food)
5. Health Concerns (weight loss, genes)
6. Media (promotion not always truthful, useful or reliable)

WATER LIMITATIONS

Water limitations are mostly geographical, but are also very much based on socioeconomic factors. Water sources often need to be treated before they reach human consumption, and methods for both collection and transport need to be created safely as well; a larger population demands larger water plants (or the like), which in turn holds larger threats to life and environment. It costs a substantial amount of money to both hire and build for safety, and even then, it cannot be guaranteed. Many disasters have been recorded due to human water demands, and if towns are able to recover, that too will cost often unreachable amounts of money & labour.

sustainability

As over-consumers, it is our responsibility to remedy the lack of equal distribution of food, and it's consequences. While one option is to simply create more food, it comes with many concerning environmental costs; and, as it stands, our increase in whole food production would not match that of population growth. Globally, poverty-stricken & food insecure communities are faced less with the lack of natural resources, but rather lacking the means to set up & implement efficient systems to harbour them; resulting in non-utilization of land. The best option, environmentally, socio-economically and MORALLY, is to invest in the implementation of safe & sustainable systems & educational resources; as set out by the 'International Conference on Nutrition (ICN)' & 'World Declaration on Nutrition (UN, 1992)'.

While every part of the world is different, a basic sustainable farm should (along with many other factors!) include the following:

SHELTER & STORAGE

The most cost efficient form of sustainable living & farming is to having land that is both suitable for human & animal dwelling, and ecological growth. In order to have liveable land, there must be ample access to necessities like water & shelter. Utilities such as power & sewage may be 'optional' in some cases, but drastically improves quality of life. Ensuring adequate storage for agricultural products is also very important.

CULTIVATION & BIODIVERSITY

Biological diversity in crops & animals protects from total loss, maximizes natural pest control (and thereby minimizing pesticide use), provides a more balanced ecosystem, & provides more dependable sustainability.

Many global sustainability models suggest a farm have the following:

- Sustainable Timber
- Wetlands
- Orchard
- Pasture
- Crop Fields

NOTE: it is best to have a minimum of 2 crop fields that rotate each year. This protects against long term loss & soil erosion.

LIVESTOCK

Livestock, like us, also need to be provided with an abundant source of clean water, shelter to protect from the elements & predators, and access to nutritionally fulfilling food. Diversity in livestock will provide food insurance, and a fertilizing & disposal system for crop.

international food trade

WHAT IS

THE 'INTERNATIONAL FOOD TRADE' REFERS TO THE GLOBAL MARKET OF IMPORTS, EXPORTS & TRADES OF FOOD PRODUCTS. EXPORTS INDICATES OUTPUT, IMPORT IS INTAKE, & TRADE REFERS TO MUTUAL EXCHANGE. BECAUSE THE FOOD TRADE IS GLOBAL, UNIVERSALLY ENFORCED POLICIES ARE NON-ATTAINABLE, AND STANDARDS ARE DEPENDANT ON COUNTRIES VOLUNTEERING TO PARTICIPATE IN, & ABIDE TO, POLICIES SET OUT BY GLOBAL PROGRAMS. THE 'FOOD AND AGRICULTURE ORGANIZATION OF THE UNITED NATIONS' & THE 'WORLD TRADE ORGANIZATION' PARTNERED & PRODUCED, THE 'TRADE AND FOOD STANDARDS'; ONE OF THE WORLD'S MOST WELL RECOGNIZED & RESPECTED SET OF STANDARDS.

HISTORY

WE CAN DATE FORMS OF TRADE BACK TO THE EARLIEST DAYS OF HUMAN INHABITATION, EVOLVING THROUGH THE YEARS OF EXPLORATION. LONG BEFORE TECHNOLOGY & NAME BRANDS, HUMANS DEPENDED ON EARTH'S NATURAL RESOURCES FOR FOOD, SHELTER, MEDICINE & CLOTHING, AND ATTAINING SUCH NECESSITIES WAS DEPENDANT ON BUILDING TIES AND BREAKING DEALS WITH THOSE THAT HAD RESOURCE ACCESS.

LIMITATIONS & PRICING

PRICING OF PRODUCT TYPICALLY DEPENDS ON A NUMBER OF FACTORS:

- LOCATION & ACCESS
- ADEQUATE SUPPLY
- DISTRIBUTION COSTS
- LIMITATIONS/RISK
- CONSUMER DEMAND
- COMPETITION/AVAILIBILITY

& CAN FLUCTUATE FOR A NUMBER OF REASONS, INCLUDING:

- CIVIL UNREST
- INTERRUPTION IN DISTRIBUTION SYSTEM
- WORKER STRIKE
- ENVIRONMENTAL/WEATHER FACTORS
- PRODUCT COMPROMISED

TOP EXPORTERS

BEEF - BRAZIL
AVOCADO - MEXICO
BANANAS - ECUADOR
ORANGES - EGYPT
SALMON - USA
CANDY - GERMANY
BLK. PEPPER - ETHIOPIA
WATER - CHINA

SOCIO-ECONOMIC

EVEN SELF-SUSTAINABLE COUNTRIES WILL USUALLY PARTICIPATE IN THE GLOBAL TRADE MARKET IN SOME FORM. THE ABILITY TO PROTECT HUMAN RIGHTS, AND FOR GOVERNEMNT ENTITIES TO OFFER ADEQUATE EDUCATION, HEALTHCARE & HOUSING (..ETC) DEPENDS GREATLY ON THE COUNTRY HAVING A SOURCE OF REVENUE. WITHOUT THIS, EITHER QUALITY OF LIFE WILL DETERIORATE, OR THE RESPONSIBILITY WILL FALL SOLELY ON A POPULATION, USUALLY BY WAY OF TAXES. THIS CAN ACCOUNT FOR THE UNPARALLELED STATISTICS OF EXPORT VS. PRODUCTION.

...what is... 'FAIR TRADE'

"..'Fairtrade' is an independent, third party certification system for goods that are produced in the Global South."

It's mission is primarily to protect producers at risk of exploitation, whether it be financial or in the workplace. 'Fair Trade' Products could bear one of a number of different stamps or marks, but one will likely be consistent in your area. Try to research your local organization, and what it's certification guarantees.

FLO (INTERNATIONAL FAIR TRADE) MARK

certifies that:

- Fairtrade is 50% owned by producers
- Fairtrade Minimum Price - Payment of the Minimum Price is regularly audited and checked by FLOCERT
- Fairtrade Premium - Over and above the Fairtrade Minimum Price, the Fairtrade Premium is an additional sum of money which goes into a communal fund for workers and farmers to use - as they see fit - to improve their social, economic and environmental conditions. Producers determine what is most important to them
- Fair price paid to producers
- High standard of human rights
- Safe working conditions
- Prohibition of child labour

www.fairtrade.net

There are many 'Fair Trade' entities, but the largest is the International Fair Trade (or FLO).

Fairtrade International unites over 25 labelling initiatives across Europe, Japan, North America, Mexico & Australia/New Zealand, as well as networks of producer organizations from Asia, Africa, Latin America and the Caribbean.

'FAIRTRADE CANADA' IS THE CANADIAN MEMBER OF INTERNATIONAL FAIR TRADE

ELIGIBILITY

Each entity/organization can have it's own eligibility requirements to be a part of their Fair Trade program, but most are very comparable.

Fair Trade Producers must meet certain social, economic and environmental standards, which basically ensures that values are aligned, and that the producers themselves are also of honest intent; in exchange for certain protection of standards.

A 'Producer" is either a small-scale farmer organization, or plantations depending on size, products, and operations.

Eligibility for a plantation and for small-scale organizations differ, as does their protected standards. Visit your local organization for more!

'Hunger' - persons living with food insecurity
'Infant Mortality' is per 1000 live births
'Life Expectency' is for the average female, in years
'Average Annual Income' is per person, adult, averaged
'Healthcare' is per person, per year, averaged
All in USD$ for easier comparison

AROU
WO

CANADA

Hunger %: 4.9 (see below)   Average BMI: 29.4
33% of Aboriginal off-reserve persons
70% of Nunavut pre-schoolers
Infant Mortality: 4.25   Poverty %: 10.5
Average Life Expectancy: 82.24
Average Annual Income $: 41,280
Healthcare $: 4,994

UNITED STATES

Hunger %: 9.8   Average BMI: 36.2
Infant Mortality: 5.56
Average Life Expectancy: 78.5
Average Annual Income $: 43,585
Healthcare $: 10,623
Poverty %: 11

CUBA

Hunger %: 2.7   Average BMI: 24.6
Infant Mortality: 3.81
Average Life Expectancy: 77.76
Average Annual Income $: 879
Healthcare $: 986.9
Poverty %: 26

Hunger %:   Average BMI:
Infant Mortality:
Average Life Expectancy:
Average Annual Income $:
Healthcare $:
Poverty %:

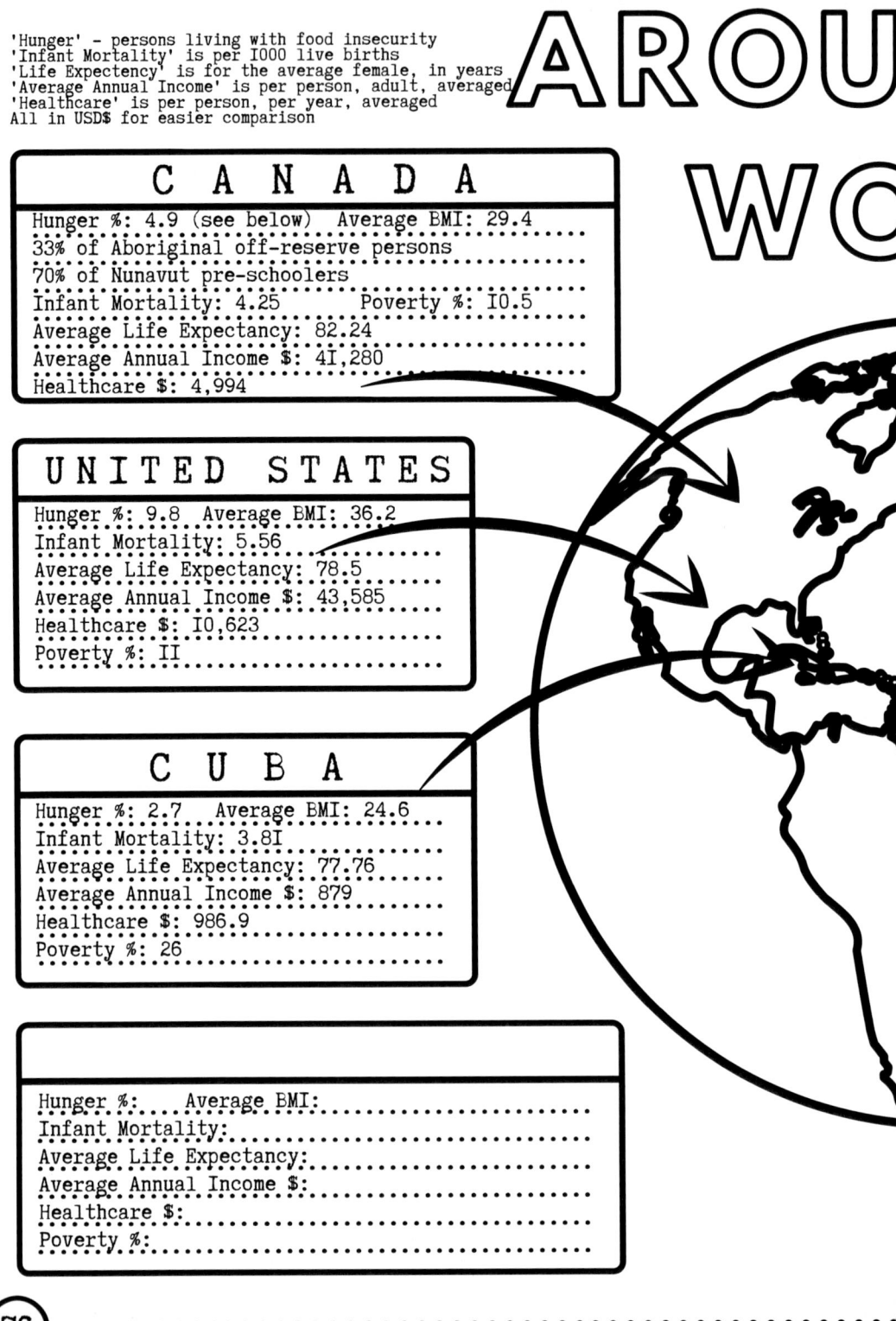

76

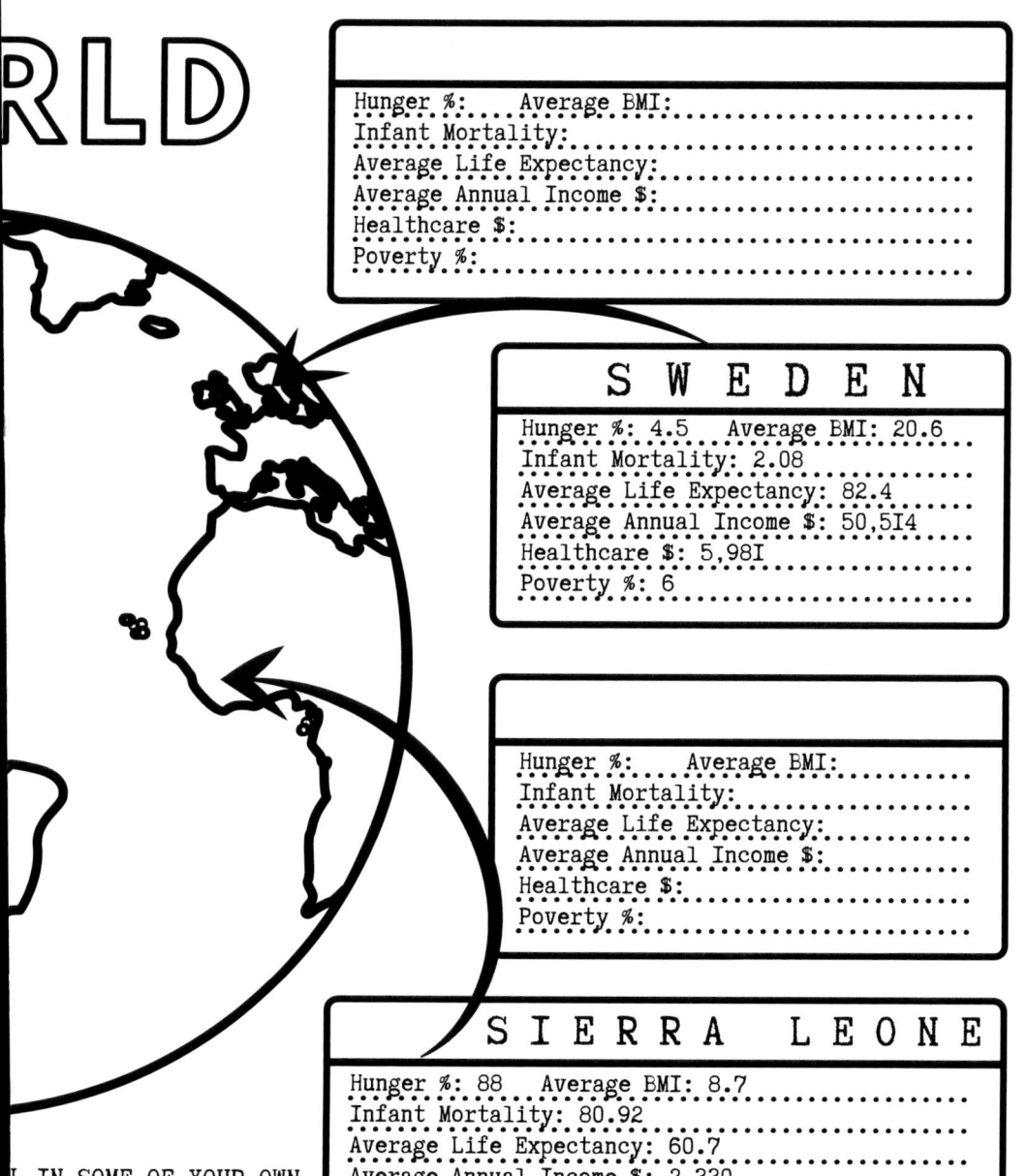

Hunger %: Average BMI:
Infant Mortality:
Average Life Expectancy:
Average Annual Income $:
Healthcare $:
Poverty %:

S W E D E N

Hunger %: 4.5 Average BMI: 20.6
Infant Mortality: 2.08
Average Life Expectancy: 82.4
Average Annual Income $: 50,514
Healthcare $: 5,981
Poverty %: 6

Hunger %: Average BMI:
Infant Mortality:
Average Life Expectancy:
Average Annual Income $:
Healthcare $:
Poverty %:

S I E R R A   L E O N E

Hunger %: 88 Average BMI: 8.7
Infant Mortality: 80.92
Average Life Expectancy: 60.7
Average Annual Income $: 2,330
Healthcare $: 85.78
Poverty %: 60

L IN SOME OF YOUR OWN
FIRST EXPLORE:
www.who.int
.globalhungerindex.org

IMPACT OF HUMAN DEMANDS ON EARTH

This beautiful planet we call home has provided us with so many wonderful flavours and resources, but, as with all things human, it has become over populated and exploited; leading to a problematic strain on the Earth and it's remaining inhabitants.

Human damage on the Earth is often consciously attributed to things like construction and industrial growth; but do you know of all the ways in which our Planet is hurting from our food demands?

- Exploitation of resources
- Destruction of ecosystems
- Reduction of trees leading to compromised air quality
- Pollution from factories and transportation
- Pollution from packaging - both garbage and during packaging production
- Hunt for Exotic/Luxurious foods and flavours only amplifies these issues, as there is typically less regard for consequences

SUSTAINABLE RESOURCES

As the human population grows so does our demand on Earth provided resources. Many of these resources are sustainable, or renewable, and will therefor regrow or regenerate. However, every year we 'use up' these resources earlier and earlier; meaning the rest of the year, we are simply depleting the Earth beyond any capacity to regenerate.

This is both unnecessary and avoidable, if we all do our part & take responsibility for our actions. You will learn of many ways to do this throughout the rest of this book, but take the time to further educate yourself, your family and your community.

IMPACT OF HUMAN DEMANDS ON ANIMALS

In the air, birds must face obstructions like taller buildings & structures, power lines, and even flying garbage, as well as pollution from factories and transportation.

Meanwhile, down on the ground, our fellow animals are competing against humans taking over their habitats, threatening food supply, & fundamentally destructing ecosystems. Consequently, with the added luring scent of garbage, wild animals are often known to come into human populations in search of food; a confrontation that rarely comes out in favour of the wild. If animals are able to avoid interactions with humans, interactions with garbage also comes with its own dangers. Transportation of food, by train or road vehicles, also claims the lives of many; humans included.

Our Oceans' animals don't fare much better than their ground or air-dwelling neighbours. Due to sheer size and physical boundaries, it is much more difficult to police waters, making oceanic creatures more prone to poaching, over hunting, and to becoming collateral damage of unethical fishing procedures. Oceanic animals must also suffer through pollution from spills, boats, garbage and sewage, usually without the ability to escape. In addition to this, most oceanic creatures feed off of the 'bottom-feeders', like shrimp and crustaceans, who (like their name suggests) are feeding off of the garbage and sewer sitting at the bottom of the seas.

COWS

The cow is, along with deer and goat, a member of a class of animals called RUMINANTS. These animals have systems designed to digest things like hay & grass (roughage); with food entering through their mouth, then down the esophagus & into the RUMEN. This digestive organ can hold up to 50 gallons, and is filled with fluid and microbes, which are resposible for much of the initial digestion of food. It is then passed through to the RETICULUM, then the OMASUM, and finally through the ABOMASUM before makes it's way into the small intestines for nutrient absorption. It is the Rumen, Reticulum, Omasum and Abomasum that gives cows '4 stomachs', but it is the Abomasum that is the 'true stomach'; performing most simularly to ours.

G R A Z E R

As you have probably already seen, cows wander through pastures and fields, munching and pooping at will. This is because they are 'grazers', but also due to the fact they are not typically 'wild', and have the luxury of not having to worry too much about potential predators; although we know that this safety and ample food comes at the ultimate price later on..

TIGERS

The carnivorous (meat-eating) tigers may have different nutritional needs and diet than humans, but shares the same general digestive system as most mammals. They have an esophagus, stomach, colon, small and large intestines, and, as with humans, digestion starts in the mouth, continues in the stomach and small intestine, and concludes with feces.

HUNTER

Tigers are, like most wild cats, PREDATORS. Their athleticism, sharp weapons and sharper senses make them extremely effective hunters. Tigers will typically have a diet of small to medium mammals, such as deer, buffalo and wild boar, but have the ability to effectively hunt much larger mammals. Tigers can and do eat up to 40kg of meat per sitting, and will typically keep their kill in a safe place to return to over several days.

TEETH

A tiger's jaw consists of 16 upper and 14 lower teeth, with some growing up to 3" long. Designed perfectly for a carnivore, they play a vital role in the hunt and digestion of food.

TWO-TOED SLOTH

The two-toed sloth lives in the rainforests of Central and South America and, unlike its three-toed herbivore cousin, is an OMNIVORE. These furry guys spend most of their time up in treetops, using their long claws to hang for hours.

Sloths are one of the least athletic of Earth's creatures, with odd claws, disproportionate limbs, and bad eyesight; but Mother Nature never makes mistakes! They are so well designed for tree dwelling that most even give birth while hanging in the canopies!

Sloths often sleep between 15-20 hours a day!! How do you think this is affected by their diet?

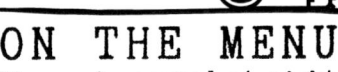

ON THE MENU

Dinner is served at night for these dozy mammals! Despite the fact they are omnivores, the typical two-toed sloth's plate consists mostly of leaves, shoots and fruit from trees, which give them both their nutritional and water needs. Their weak legs and long claws make it difficult to get around on land, and their lack of agility make them defenseless to attacks from predators like wild cats and birds of prey, making it harder to get their furry hands on yummy, energy-packed bugs & insects.

RANDOM FACT

The two-toed sloth is one of the world's slowest mammals; so slow, in fact, that algae grows on their fur!! It's green tint provides the sloths with camouflage up in the trees; another example of a SYMBIOTIC relationship!

NUTRITIONAL HEALTH

THE OPTIMAL DIET HAS VARIETY, BALANCE, MODERATION & CALORIE CONTROL; SOUNDS EASY ENOUGH RIGHT? BUT, JUST LIKE YOUR TEETH, YOU SHOULD STILL BE CHECKING IN WITH YOURSELF AND, WHEN INDICATED, A DOCTOR TO MAKE SURE YOU'RE HEALTHY AND THRIVING!

By now, you already know of a few factors that can contribute to, or take from, your nutritional well-being, including your genes, allergies and physical demands. Some may be very obvious and manageable, while others can be quite hard to diagnose or even notice. Your body will do a lot to try and compensate for any deficits, so usually, by the time you see symptoms, it is already advanced & with long term effects (refer to page 70). As much as the damage of malnutrition doesn't happen in a day, neither does it's repair; so nutritional health truly is a lifestyle. Afterall, you can do a DRAMATIC amount of health improvement by way of nutrition, because..

BIOCHEMICALLY, YOU ARE WHAT YOU EAT

DID YOU KNOW?

Nutrition is a KEY factor in 3 of top 10 causes of death:
- Cancer
- Heart Disease
- Stroke

Diets high in WHOLE GRAINS shows a reduction in Heart Disease.

NUTRIGENOMICS

..is the study of the relationship/interactions between genes & nutrition.

Genes are built up o proteins that DEFINE genetic interactions. This basically means your genes have prewritten messages missions when interacting with nutrition; and these interaction outcomes ar what defines your risk o suffering from certain medical conditions. For example: A specific gene reduces your body' ability to secrete sodiu optimally; lack of sodiu puts you at risk of hig blood pressure. (Page 40)

ASSESSING NUTRITIONAL HEALTH

From the day you were born, the people around you have been meticulously tracking your health and planning your nutrition for optimal growth. Throughout your life, you will have 'health markers' monitored like weight & height, and organ function & development, but Doctors and adults will pay extra close attention during childhood. Can you guess why? RIGHT! You are GROWING! Growing so fast, that your body must consume all the nourishment it needs, so any kind of deficit or needed medical intervention must be caught as early as possible. Don't worry, though! Symptoms of nutritional issues are much easier to catch while you are young and developing, as not only are they more prevalent than they would be in an adult, but there has been substantial research in child development making it very easy to detect if you are out of any Optimal Health and Development Ranges, and make the necessary dietary or lifestyle changes.

WAYS TO ASSESS NUTRITIONAL HEALTH

- Weight/Height (BMI)
- Blood Testing
- Urine Samples
- Stool Samples
- Organ Function
- Growth Rates
- Allergy Testing
- Diet Tracking
- Spit Testing
- Body Scans
- Mental Health
- Physical Exams
- Nutrigenomics

..and many more!

AS YOU GROW

As you grow up, the responsibility of your nutrition and health begins to fall into your own hands. While you don't have access to the same testing as a doctor, the best way to keep yourself on track is to learn to listen to your body with the aid of Food Tracking. See page 96.

NUTRITION FOR MEDICINE

SINCE THE DAWN OF TIME, EARTH-DWELLERS HAVE BEEN USING SURROUNDING NATURAL RESOURCES FOR CLOSE TO EVERYTHING, INCLUDING AS MEDICINE. WHILE INVESTMENT AND AWARENESS IN YOUR NUTRITIONAL HEALTH IS HEALING IN & OF ITSELF, THE THINGS YOU SEE AS FOOD HAVE BEEN FOUND TO HAVE HEALING PROPERTIES BY WAY OF INGESTION, TOPICAL APPLICATION OR OTHERWISE, AND HAVE BEEN USED THIS WAY FOR CENTURIES. OVER TIME, THESE NATURAL REMEDIES HAVE BEEN REPLACED WITH ARTIFICIAL 'EQUIVALENTS', BUT DON'T WORRY, I'LL BET YOU USE MORE NATURAL REMEDIES THAN YOU'VE EVER NOTICED!

NATUROPATHY VS PHARMACEUTICALS

NATUROPATHY REFERS TO MEDICINAL TREATMENTS CONSISTING OF NATURAL REMEDIES WITH INTENT OF PROMOTING SELF-HEALING. PHARMACEUTICALS ARE DRUGS CREATED AND DEVELOPED FOR 'MEDICINAL PURPOSES' THAT ARE TYPICALLY CHEMICAL IN NATURE.

INFLAMMATION

Inflammation is just one of the body's immune responses, whereby white blood cells surround at-risk or damaged cells, resulting in what topi-cally presents as redness & swelling. Acute inflammation refers to the body's immune response to injury or infec-tion and is a necessary & healthy part of your healing process. Chronic inflammation, however, is defined by unwar-ranted long-lasting inflam-mation symptoms, which leads to an overworked immune system and could result in white blood cells attacking healthy tissue. Long term effects of chronic inflammation have been linked to heart disease, diabetes, cancer, arthritis & multiple bowel diseases. Chronic inflammation is just one of the many ailments that can be linked to nutrition.

ILLNESS/WELLNESS CONTINUUM

HIGH LEVEL AWARENESS
∧
GROWTH
∧
EDUCATION
∧
AWARENESS
∧
NEUTRAL POINT
no discernible illness or wellness
∨
SIGNS
∨
SYMPTOMS
∨
DISABILITY
∨
PREMATURE DEATH

Turmeric

A natural antiseptic & antibiotic agent, Turmeric has been used for years for its medicinal properties. It also contains collagen moderating properties, that aid in topical healing.

Use: If the wound is actively bleeding, apply turmeric directly on the wound; bleeding will cease. Drinking turmeric milk before bed has also proven to drastically improve healing time & recovery.

Garlic

Garlic has been known for its anti-microbial and antibiotic properties for centuries. It can aid in clotting on active trauma bleeds, reduce pain and promote healing by boosting the body's natural defences.

Use: On an active-bleed wound, apply a few crushed garlic cloves.

Honey

Honey is well known for its anti-bacterial, anti-fungal and anti-inflammatory properties.

Use: Apply honey directly on the wound regularly before washing it.

Limestone powder

Limestone powder (also known as Chuna) is commonly used in paan, & has many healing properties.

Use: Mix Turmeric & Limestone powder, and put over heat. Once well mixed, apply directly to the wound and allow to air dry, or heat a towel with warm water and lay over the wound, let sit until towel gets cold, then wipe.

Aloe Vera

Aloe Vera has analgesic, anti-inflammatory and soothing properties that aid in the healing process. Aloe gel contains phytochemicals that can reduce pain and inflammation.

Use: Cut open an aloe vera leaf and extract the gel. Apply the gel on the wound and let it dry. Clean the area with warm water & pat dry with a clean towel.

Coconut oil

With moisturizing, anti-inflammatory & anti-bacteria properties, coconut oil works as both a pain reliever and helps protect against infection. It can also be very effective in reducing scarring.

Use: Apply oil on the affected area and cover with a clean cloth. Re-apply the coconut oil at least 2-3 times daily.

Onion

Onion contains an anti-microbial compound called allicin that helps to protect wounds from infection.

Use: Blend an onion and honey in a blender until you get a paste. Apply it directly over the wound to accelerate the healing process.

WARNING
NEVER TAKE ANYONE'S -INCLUDING YOUR OWN- MEDICAL CARE INTO YOUR OWN HANDS. ALWAYS GO TO A PROFESSIONAL!!!

ANTIOXIDANTS

oxidization

'Oxidization' (in relation to antioxidants in nutrition) refers to the damage caused to cells by 'Free Radicals'. Free radicals are naturally produced in our body, as both a byproduct of energy metabolization & usage, and also from less ideal sources like smoking & air pollution. Your body controls and maintains unavoidable free radical production with 'antioxidants'; typically via our food. Free radicals cause destruction by chomping up electrons from surrounding cells, consequently changing and weakening their structure & functions. When in excess, free radicals can have detrimental effects if left un-challenged long term. ANTIOXIDANTS work by providing an influx of electrons, which stops the free radicals needs to cause damage to its neighbouring cells as they are no longer hungry. Over the years, our exposure to free radical sources have dramatically increased, which in turn means so must our efforts to consume enough antioxidant-rich food!

abundant sources

Look for foods containing high amounts of: Selenium, Zinc, Iron, Manganese, Vitamin E & Beta-Carotene.

BLUEBERRIES - DARK CHOCOLATE - RASPBERRIES - GOJI BERRIES
KALE - PECANS - STRAWBERRIES - KIWI - LEMON - BELL PEPPER
BROCCOLI - BEETS - COLLARD GREENS - CANTALOUPE - TOMATOES

IMMUNITY

Your body has it's own built in defense system that protects you from bad intruders like germs and viruses that carry disease, infection and sickness (like the flu!). This defence system is called your IMMUNE system, and it needs to be strong & thriving to protect you from threats effectively, including balance, abundance, hydration and, of course, complete nutrition. There are two general ways in which your immunity will work to protect you:

1. DEFEND

- Enhancement of antioxidant synthesis (phagocytosis)
- Changing form of cell structure

Additionally, our immune system will remember harmful organisms!

2. ATTACK

- Engulfing of harmful organisms by 'Phagocytes'
- Destruction of already infected cells by the binding of cytotoxic T-cells

MINDFUL EATING

LISTEN TO YOUR BODY

WHAT IS INTUITIVE EATING?

Intuitive eating is a 'style' of eating that promotes SELF REGULATION of your hunger and nutritional choices, based on your own body's signals and needs. This means getting to know your body, your moods, your responses and reactions to certain foods and food types. Intuitive eating is the key to optimal health; but it is a learned power. (Page 96)

BALANCE IS KEY

FOOD FOR FUEL

The first step on your road to optimal nutritional health, is understanding that the food you eat is PRIMARILY your body's source of fuel, and, just like a car, the amount of fuel you put in your body will determine how far you can go, and the quality of that fuel makes a difference in how long your 'engine' lasts..

You, just like a car, are lots of systems running independently and simultaneously, each playing a role in making the WHOLE machine operate optimally. A car has an engine, like you have a heart, it has a computer system that serves as it's 'brain', headlights that work optimally when they are clear and bright, and a stereo system as loud and controllable as your voice! A car is full of tubes that transport fluids, which must stay clean to avoid dangerous build up and blockage, and signals and codes that tell each system when it is needed and how hard it must work. If one system goes, the entire machine is compromised. It is important to remember to choose:

NUTRIENT FULFILLMENT FIRST,
FOOD SATISFACTION SECOND.

So, make sure you have enough and the right kinds of fuel in your tank! Every activity you do (even sleeping!) requires energy, and that energy comes from your food. Go to page 41 for more smart energy choices.

low quality food = low quality fuel

ABC'S OF NUTRITION

ABUNDANCE
PLENTIFUL FULFILNESS

It is often believed that healthy eating is about restrictions and limitations, but that is so very far from the truth!! The Key to Health is abundance.. of variety, culture, colour and joy; all of which can be found, fueled or explored through your food & nutrition.

BALANCE
A STATE OF EQUILIBRIUM

The key to all things in life is finding a healthy balance; Too much of anything, even the great stuff, is not always good; so, eat your favourite foods, celebrate and love life, but do it all within reason. Studies show that the best ratio for balance is 80:20, which means you should aim to make the 'best' decisions 80% of the time, and to give yourself a little bit of a break the other 20%. Luckily for us, we are starting to learn of so many ways we can make the 'bad' things we love 'good', which means not only would your healthy balance look more like 90:10, but you will be...

THRIVING NOT DEPRIVING!

CREATION
ART OF IMAGINATION

Imagination & Creativity are as essential to your quality of life as the people you surround yourself with. It can be easy to get lost in the science and the numbers, but having a good relationship with food is vital, and you should LOVE the things that fuel your body, so

CREATE, EXPLORE, SHARE AND HAVE FUN!

COLOURS OF FOOD

RED	LYCOPENE MAY LOWER RISK OF HEART DISEASE AND PROSTATE CANCER
YELLOW	LUTEIN AND ZEAXANTHIN ARE BOTH IMPORTANT FOR EYE ANTI-AGING.
PINK	CONTAINS VITAMIN C, FOLATE, FLAVINOIDS, AND TANNIN, WHICH PROTECT OUR CELLS FROM BACTERIA
GREEN	ISOTHIOCYANTES CAN HELP PREVENT CANCER. MOST BENEFICIAL WHEN RAW
ORANGE	CAROTENOIDS TURN INTO VITAMIN A, WHICH IS NEEDED FOR CELL GROWTH, VISION & HEALTHY IMMUNE FUNCTION
PURPLE	ANTHOCYANINS, ANTIOXIDANTS THAT CAN HELP REDUCE INFLAMMATION
BLUE	ANTIOXIDANTS HAVE PROVEN TO HELP FIGHT AGAINST AUTOIMMUNE DISEASES
BLACK	ANTHOCYANINS HELP MAKE YOUR SKIN GLOW, AND HAVE MANY ANTI-AGING AND DETOXIFYING PROPERTIES
WHITE	ALLIUMS CONTAIN ORGANOSULFUR, WHICH CAN PROTECT AGAINST STOMACH AND COLORECTAL CANCERS

THE MOST NUTRIENT DENSE MEALS WILL HAVE AT LEAST 3 COLOURS OF THE RAINBOW

A SIMPLE GUIDE TO
TRACKING NUTRITION

Tracking nutrition can be a great tool for your optimal health journey, IF done in a way that is exactly that.. healthy! Follow this simple guide for Nutrition and Food Tracking Success!

FOR POSITIVE REASONS ONLY

Your food journal should only be used as a tool to improve your quality of life, relationship with food, or your health. While you may sometimes use it to hold yourself accountable, do not lose sight of the fact you are doing this because you are worthy of investment, and deserve health and happiness.

INTUITIVE EATING 'TRAINING'

Food journal's are one of the best ways to begin learning to Listen To Your Body. Tracking your food and it's nutrient content will help you identify links to how you're feeling, what you might be missing from your diet, and what your body does when it's trying to tell you what it needs. If you are still feeling hungry after meals, or tired throughout the day (even after full sleeps) a food journal could really help you. There are many ways to find out the nutrient content of the foods you are eating, some apps and websites allow you to scan barcodes of food products, or search individual ingredients to build your meal. TIP: Try doing this for the meals you consume often to save yourself time, and give you a place to start. Don't forget to take notes on how you are feeling during the day, as well as after meals & snacks.

ELIMINATE INTOLERANCES & ALLERGIES

A food journal is likely the first thing a Doctor will ask you to do to try and identify any food intolerances, sensitivities or allergies. Just like 'intuitive eating training', you should take note of everything you eat, but instead of focusing mostly on nutritional values, you should pay closer attention to ingredients. It is important to take note of the times you eat and of when symptoms of intolerance happen, and how you feel!

NEVER CHANGE YOUR NUTRITIONAL INTAKE BEFORE SPEAKING WITH A GUARDIAN OR DOCTOR

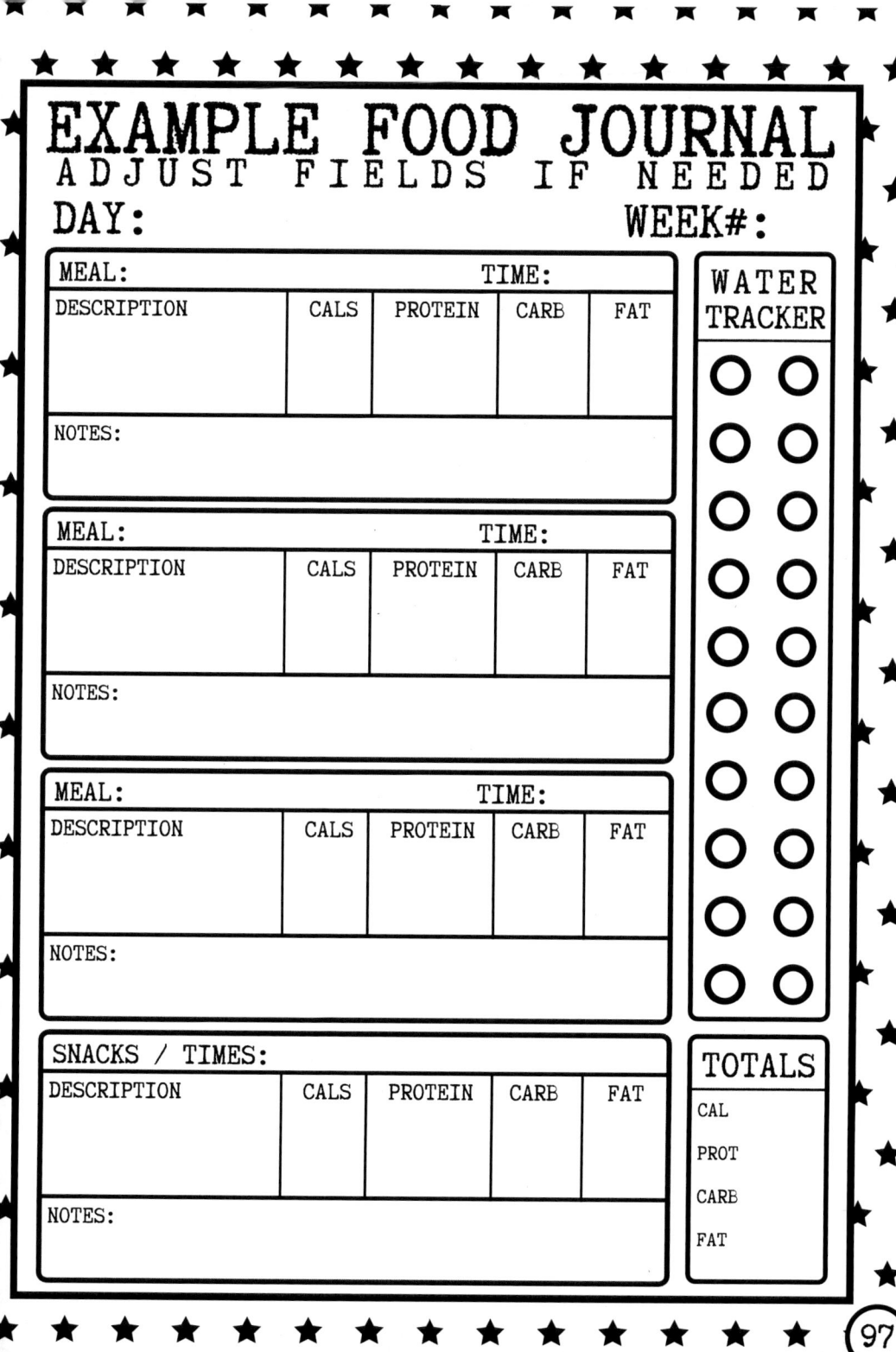

COST OF CONVENIENCE

**$/SPEED SAVED FOR YOU, IS
$/SPEED SAVED IN PRODUCTION**

1 POOR NUTRIENT DENSITY

Poor Nutrient Density, or 'Empty Calories' refers to the amount of nutrients per calories you are consuming. For example - KIWI vs. CAN OF SODA - both use up a similar amount of your daily calories, but the kiwi contains MULTIPLE additional and powerful nutrients.

2 PRODUCTION CUTS

In order to offer low prices, cuts are made in both the quality of production and quality of the food itself. These cuts are often at the expense of ethical values. (pg 56 & 75)

3 ADDITIVES AND PRESERVATIVES

Things like 'additives' and 'preservatives' are added into our foods & drinks for a few reasons, but usually for taste, appeal, or to extend shelf life. (page 48)

4 LOSS OF SKILLS & LEARNING

One of the more overlooked costs of convenience, is the loss of the kitchen skills that would usually be taught or passed down as you grow up. This is largely due to longer work and school days.

CARBONATED BEVERAGES AKA POP

Pop, or soda, not only contains HIGH levels of sugar (or worse), but most also contains multiple unsafe chemicals. Keep an eye on ingredient lists, as many contain 'things' like High Fructose Corn Syrup, Brominated Vegetable Oil (ingredient in toxic flame retardant) and Polydimethylsiloxane (silly putty).

MAKING THINGS SWEETER

MOLASSES / BROWN SUGAR

Molasses is a dark, thick syrup that is a byproduct of the process of making white sugar from sugar cane.

Brown sugar is the result of adding some molasses <u>back</u> into white sugar.

GRANULATED SUGAR

Granulated sugar, also known as white sugar or sucrose, is made from sugar cane. Cane syrup is extracted, filtered and crystalized to create this common choice. It has less mineral content with the molasses removed.

SYRUPS / SWEETENERS

Many syrups are natural & are usually the better choice, however, some are made from the same ingredients as many artificial sweeteners .. so the best thing to do (as always) is to read & research ingredients.

NATURAL ALTERNATIVES

- HONEY
- MAPLE SYRUP
- COCONUT AMINOS
- AGAVE NECTAR
- DATES
- LUCUMA
- DEHYDRATED FRUIT POWDERS

FRUCTOSE

FRUCTOSE IS NATURALLY FOUND IN THINGS LIKE FRUIT AND HONEY, AND IS OFTEN CALLED FRUIT SUGAR; <u>BUT BE WARNED</u>, 'HIGH-FRUCTOSE CORN SYRUP' IS NOT THE SAME. THERE IS SUBSTANTIAL RESEARCH TO SHOW THIS FORM OF SWEETENER HAS MULTIPLE NEGATIVE EFFECTS ON YOUR BODY & MIND, SO STEER CLEAR WHEN POSSIBLE.

WARNING: SWEETENERS AFFECT BLOOD GLUCOSE LEVELS DIFFERENTLY (P.44)

MORE THAN FOOD

Food is a crazy thing! Sometimes, the things you think of as food, can be used for many other things! Whether it's as a cleaner, a medicine, a paint or a beauty product, the things nature gives us can go so much further than our bellies!

COCONUT OIL	FOOD	SKIN
	Coconut oil is a good source of Medium Chain Fatty Acids & can improve brain function!	Coconut oil is great for skin, as it can help with both acne and inflammation issues! (see page 84)

VINEGAR	FOOD	CLEANER
	Vinegar can add flavour and texture to foods, and there are many kinds to choose from!	White Vinegar can be diluted with water to make a natural, non-toxic, grime cutting, bacteria killer!

HOWEVER

IT CAN BE SO FUN TO FIND ALL THE DIFFERENT WAYS NATURE CAN BE USED, HOWEVER, THERE ARE MANY THINGS AROUND OUR HOMES WITH INGREDIENTS THAT ARE ARTIFICIAL AND WE SHOULD <u>NOT</u> BE CONSUMING, BUT THAT <u>ARE</u> IN OUR FOOD. GROSS, RIGHT? SEE IF YOU CAN GUESS WHICH INGREDIENTS BELOW ARE FROM FOOD, AND WHICH ARE FROM ANOTHER HOUSEHOLD ITEM.

1.

A OR B

INGREDIENTS
SUGAR, CORN SYRUP, SHELLAC, SALT, DEXTROSE, GELATIN, SESAME OIL, ARTIFICIAL FLAVOR, HONEY, YELLOW 6, YELLOW 5, RED 3

INGREDIENTS
WATER, SODIUM LAURETH SULFATE, COCAMIDOPROPYL BETAINE, PHENOXYETHANOL, GLYCOL DISTEARATE, CITRIC ACID, CALENDULA OFFICINALIS FLOWER EXTRACT, RED #4, YELLOW #5, BLUE #1, ALOE.

2.

A OR B

INGREDIENTS
PIPERONYL BUTOXIDE, PYRETHRUM EXTRACT, AMMONIUM LAURETH SULFATE, DEHYDRATED ALCOHOL, FRAGRANCE, ISOPROPYL ALCOHOL, PEG-25 HYDROGENATED CASTOR OIL, POLYQUATERNIUM-10, WATER

INGREDIENTS
HIGH FUCTOSE CORN SYRUP, DISTILLED VINEGAR. VEGETABLE OIL, WATER, SUGAR, MALTODEXTRIN, XANTHAN GUM, TITANIUM DIOXIDE, POTASSIUM SORBATE, CALCIUM DISODIUM EDTA, YELLOW #5

1A: 'Candy Corn'. 1B: Face Wash. 2A: Lice Shampoo. 2B: Ranch Dressing.

BE HEALTHIER

5 STEPS TO BUILDING A HEALTHIER LIFESTYLE

1 DO YOUR FIRST FOOD JOURNAL

THE BEST WAY TO FIGURE OUT HOW YOU SHOULD BE ADJUSTING YOUR DIET, IS TO DO A FOOD JOURNAL. YOU NEED IT TO BE BOTH TRUTHFUL AND A TYPICAL DAY FOR YOU. TRY FOR 7 DAYS

2 MAKE A LIST OF YOUR FAVOURITES

THERE IS NO REASON YOU NEED TO CHOOSE BETWEEN "HEALTHY" & THE FOODS YOU LOVE. START A LIST OF YOUR FAVOURITE MEALS AND TRY TO MAKE NEW RECIPES WITH A FEW HEALTHY SWAP-OUTS!

3 MAKE SMALL STEPS OVER TIME

SLOW AND STEADY REALLY IS THE ANSWER TO ACHIEVING HEALTH & HAPPINESS. IT ALLOWS YOUR MIND AND BODY TO ADJUST AT A SAFE PACE, AND ALSO GIVES YOU A CHANCE TO REALLY FOCUS ON WHAT YOUR BODY RUNS BEST OFF OF!!

4 ENJOY FOOD

IT IS SO VERY IMPORTANT THAT YOU MAINTAIN A HEALTHY RELATIONSHIP WITH FOOD. ENJOY YOUR MEALS AND TAKE TIME TO APPRECIATE IT'S FLAVOURS & BLESSINGS.. LIFE IS ALL ABOUT BALANCE!!

5 INCLUDE YOUR LOVED ONES

INVOLVING YOUR LOVED ONES IN YOUR NUTRITION HAS A NUMBER OF BENEFITS. WHEN IT COMES TO THE PEOPLE YOU LIVE WITH, IT WILL A LOT EASIER TO KEEP ON TRACK IF EVERYONE ELSE IS TOO! PLUS HELPING YOUR FAMILY BECOME HEALTHIER, STRONGER AND HAPPIER IS A TRULY BEAUTIFUL THING!!

CHEAT SHEET

FUN & HEALTHY ALTERNATIVES

INSTEAD OF	CHOOSE
CHIPS	BAKED FRUIT SLICES
ICE CREAM	FROZEN JUICE BARS
CANDY BARS	HOMEMADE POWER BARS
RANCH DIP	HOMEMADE HUMMUS
CHOCOLATE PUDDING	CHOCO-AVO PUDDING
CHEESEBURGER	HOUSEMADE BURGER
CHOC. MILKSHAKE	CHOC. SMOOTHIE
REGULAR POTATO	SWEET POTATO
CANDY	FRUIT & NUT MIX

YOU DON'T NEED TO GIVE UP YOUR FAVOURITES.. NOT ONLY IS LIFE ABOUT BALANCE AND MODERATION, BUT EVEN THE MOST "UNHEALTHY" THINGS CAN BE MADE WITH HEALTHY INGREDIENT SUBSTITUTES.

secret recipe

Homemade Power Bars

SERVES: --
TIME: 40

DIRECTIONS

1. Preheat oven to 350 F and line your baking pan with parchment paper.
2. Mix all DRY ingredients - Add oats, sweetener, spices, nuts or seeds to a large mixing bowl.
3. Add in all WET ingredients - Stir in your heated liquid binder, liquid sweetener & some pure vanilla extract. Mix until totally combined & sticky. Not swimming in liquid OR crumbling dry. (Add more ingredients if needed)
4. Spread your mixture evenly onto your baking pan and press down firmly with hands or spatula.
5. Bake at 350 for 15-20 minutes OR (for no heat recipe) chill in the freezer until fully set.
6. Allow to cool completely, Cut into bars, store & serve!

-------- YOU'LL NEED --------

- Oven
- Mixing Bowl
- Spatula
- Baking Sheet
- Parchment Paper
- Air-tight Container

INGREDIENTS

Dry coarse base: oats, shredded coconut, chopped nuts

Sticky liquid binder + sweetener: maple syrup, honey, agave nectar

Liquid binder: oil, butter, nut butter

Dry binder: flour, almond meal, flaxseeds, protein powder

Fillers: seeds, chopped nuts, chopped chocolate, dried fruit, coconut flakes, cereal

+ Pure Vanilla Extract

NUTRITIONAL INFO
PER ONE SERVING
Calories .... --
Total Fat .... --g
   Saturated ..... --g
   Trans .... --g
   Polyunsat ..... --g
   Monounsat ..... --g
Cholesterol ..... --mg
Sodium .... --mg
Total Carbs ..... --g
   Dietary Fibre . --g
   Sugar .... --g
   Added Sugars . --g
Protein .... --g
Vitamin D .... --%
Calcium .... --%
Iron .... --%
Potassium .... --mg
Vitamin A .... --%
Vitamin C .... --

secret recipe

Avo-Choco Mousse

SERVES: 8
PREP TIME: 30

DIRECTIONS

VANILLA CREAM

NOTE: Presoak cashews in water for 2 hours first, then drain.

1. Warm coconut oil in microwave or pan until liquid.
2. Place drained cashews, water, warmed oil, agave nectar and pure vanilla extract in high powered blender.
3. Blend until smooth.

AVO-CHOCO MOUSSE

Place ALL ingredients into a food processor or blender & blender 1-2 mins until smooth.
NOTE: Scrape edges or add more Avo if mixture is too thin.

PLACE BOTH MIXTURES IN THE FRIDGE FOR MIN 2 HOURS, THEN SPOON INTO YOUR GLASSES IN BEAUTIFUL LAYERS & SERVE!!

------- YOU'LL NEED --------

- BLENDER
- STRAINER
- BOWL
- SPOON
- SUNDAE GLASSES
- REFRIGERATOR

INGREDIENTS

AVO-CHOCO MOUSSE
2 large Avocados
2/3 cup cacao powder
3/4 cup agave nectar
2 tsp orange zest (optional)

VANILLA CREAM MOUSSE
1 1/2 cups soaked cashews
1/3 cup warmed coconut oil
1/3 cup water
1/3 cup agave nectar
2 tsp Pure vanilla extract

NUTRITIONAL INFO

PER ONE SERVING
Calories 482
Total Fat 26.7g
   Saturated 10.9g
   Trans 0g
   Polyunsat 2.6g
   Monounsat 10.9g
Cholesterol 0mg
Sodium 15.4mg
Total Carbs 54.2g
   Dietary Fibre . 7.3g
   Sugar 34.4g
   Added Sugars . 0g
Protein 7.3g
Vitamin D 0%
Calcium 9.7%
Iron 13.9%
Potassium 435.9mg
Vitamin A 3.6%
Vitamin C 5.2%

secret recipe

Homemade Doughnuts

SERVES: 6
TIME: 45

DIRECTIONS

1. Preheat oven to 350F and grease your doughnut pan.

2. In a bowl, combine protein, flour, baking powder and soda, salt and spices & set aside.

3. In a separate bowl combine apple cider, apple cider vinegar, coconut oil, vanilla and coconut sugar. Whisk to mix.

4. Combine wet and dry ingredients until all dry ingredients mixed. Spoon batter into greased doughnut pan and sprinkle with additional cinnamon & coconut sugar.

5. Bake for 15 to 25 minutes depending on size of doughnut pan.

6. While still warm, place doughnuts into bowl, drizzle with coconut oil and sprinkle with cinnamon & coconut sugar. Toss to coat, then SERVE.

------- YOU'LL NEED --------

- Oven
- 2 Mixing Bowls
- Whisk
- Spoon
- Donut Pan

(or mini muffin pan to make donut holes)

INGREDIENTS

- 1 serving Vega Protein & Greens Vanilla (or alt.)
- 2 cups all-purpose flour
- 2 tsp baking powder
- 1 tsp baking soda
- 1/2 tsp pink salt
- 1 tsp cinnamon
- 1/2 tsp nutmeg
- 1 cup apple cider
- 2 tsp apple cider vinegar
- 1/4 cup coconut oil
- 1 tsp vanilla extract
- 1/3 cup coconut sugar

NUTRITIONAL INFO
PER ONE SERVING

Calories	313
Total Fat	10.2g
Saturated	7.7g
Trans	0g
Polyunsat	0.2g
Monounsat	0.6g
Cholesterol	0mg
Sodium	600.8mg
Total Carbs	47g
Dietary Fibre	1.9g
Sugar	15.9g
Added Sugars	0g
Protein	7.4g
Vitamin D	0%
Calcium	95.6%
Iron	6.5%
Potassium	28.9mg
Vitamin A	1.7%
Vitamin C	2.7%

RULES TO EATING RESPONSIBLY

1. KNOW YOUR SOURCE

2. REDUCE WASTE

3. SUPPORT LOCAL

4. PLAN AND PREPARE

5. KEEP GOING!!

KNOW YOUR SOURCE

WHEN IT COMES TO YOUR HEALTH, TO YOUR FAMILY'S HEALTH, AND TO THE FOOD THAT KEEPS YOU <u>ALL</u> ALIVE AND THRIVING, YOU DESERVE TO HAVE ALL THE INFORMATION, AND YOU ARE ENTITLED TO TRUST THAT THE INFORMATION IS TRUTHFUL & TRANSPARENT.

Unfortunately, even with laws, rules and regulations working to protect us, we can't always depend or trust all sources, whether that's information or our food. This doesn't always mean people or companies are "bad" as, more often than not, the information we receive can be limited; either by knowledge, science, or people. By now, you might have already heard of some of these limitations.

Try coming up with a few questions that you can ask yourself when deciding if your source is worth your trust. Here are some examples:

- Have I heard of them before?
- What do reviews say?
- Are they making money off of my choice?
- Do their ideals & methods align with mine?
- How long have they been around?

GROCERY SHOP CHEAT SHEET

1. PREPARE & PLAN

BEING PREPARED IS THE EASIEST WAY TO STICK TO GOALS, MINIMIZE FOOD WASTE, TRACK NUTRITION, AND KNOW WHAT'S GOING INTO YOUR BODY. YOU CAN DO THIS BY PLANNING MEALS AND SNACKS, AND <u>THEN</u> SHOP FOR WHAT YOU ACTUALLY NEED FROM A LIST.

2. STAY ON YOUR MISSION

EVEN WITH YOUR GROCERY LIST, THE STORE CAN HOLD MANY TEMPTATIONS, WITH AISLES OF CANDY AND CHIPS, POP AND PIZZA, BUT THERE ARE SOME INSIDER TRICKS TO HELP YOU OUT; THE BEST ONE: MOST, IF NOT ALL, FRESH AND WHOLE FOODS ARE AROUND THE <u>OUTSIDE</u> OF GROCERY STORES, SO STICK TO THE PERIMETER, ONLY GO INTO AISLES FOR WHAT'S ON YOUR LIST, & YOU'LL DODGE TEMPTATION!

3. BRING YOUR OWN BAG!!!

BRINGING YOUR OWN BAG COULD POTENTIALLY SAVE HUNDREDS OF ANIMALS AND PLANTS OVER YOUR LIFETIME.. REALLY! BUT REMEMBERING IT.. OH, THAT'S NOT AS EASY AS IT SOUNDS! ASK YOUR FRIENDS AND FAMILY IF THEY HAVE ANY TIPS, THEN PASS THEM ALONG TO US ALL!

wasteNOT:

As you saw on page 78, waste and garbage from humans has a major impact on the world around us. In some cases, things like packaging are a little more out of your control, but, (as much as you can) follow the

3R's

Re-usable.. oooh, this is where things get really fun! Re-useable = personalized!! A shopping bag, or coffee mug, a water bottle or vegetable bags for your grocery shops.. almost everything can be improved on. (PLUS let's be real.. saving the world looks way better personalized!!)

Reduce

The easiest and most effectiv way to reduce the impacts o human waste on our beautifu planet, is to reduce ou overall waste! This means les packaging and choosing item that are designed for multipl uses. Try not to bu "disposable" products, an stick to packaging that i biodegradable, o recyclable only

TRY ANALYZIN YOUR HOME'S WAST BY SWITCHING T CLEAR GARBAG BAGS FOR WHILE!

Recycle

Sometime: things happe you forget yo mug, you need snack, yo groceries co prepackaged.. these situations, the be you can do is recycle much as possible! Mo municipality's have recycl programs, and info about eligible materials can usually be found on local sites and boards!

Re-use

TO FURTHER MINIMIZE THE IMPACT OF THE WASTE YOUR HOME DOES PRODUCE, MAKE SURE YOU KNOW WHEN (AND WHAT) YOUR MUNICIPALITY WILL PICK UP & RECYCLE FOR YOU. SET AN ALARM IF NEEDED.

NEVER FORGET: YOU ARE YOUR BODY'S GREATEST ADVOCATE

KEEP GOING

COMPOST SYSTEMS

'Compost' is organic matter (like food scraps) that is broken down naturally and over time, resulting in what is sometimes referred to as "Earth's Conditioner". Although it is technically food (and other organic materials) that has gone 'bad', and is probably stinky and kind of gross to look at, compost has an abundance of benefits for our Earth; after all, that's how Mother Nature has been dealing with her waste since the beginning of time!!

MAKING YOUR COMPOST SYSTEM

Many cities have introduced compost programs into your regular household waste pick ups; some have even reduced the amount & frequency of "garbage" they'll pick up to encourage more composting and responsible waste management. If these programs exist in your community, then you'll probably already have a new "compost" bin outside, and a smaller one in your kitchen.

If you do not have a local program, you can either make a compost system to use in your own garden or property, research local ways for you to utilize your compost (like community gardens or waste centres), or, if none of these are possible for you, even separating your compostable materials into biodegradable bags with your regular waste pick up will be a positive step towards reducing our impact on Earth and it's inhabitants. Deciding what to do with your compost is your first step, as you want to make sure you're not making something too big to move or too close to windows you regularly open. When creating your indoor compost bin, it is best to first find biodegradable bags, and then find a container, with a lid, to fit them into. Good Luck!

BE A CULTIVATOR

ONE OF THE MOST EFFECTIVE WAYS TO HELP WITH THE PRESSURE THAT HUMANS PUT ON THE EARTH AND IT'S RESOURCES, IS TO BEGIN TO TAKE MORE RESPONSIBILITY FOR THE CULTIVATION OF OUR FOOD. CREATING RENEWABLE RESOURCES ON A GLOBAL SCALE IS, OF COURSE, THE DREAM.. BUT FOR NOW, YOU CAN START BY MAKING A DIFFERENCE IN YOUR HOME! CULTIVATING YOUR OWN FOOD IS NOT ONLY FUN AND EARTH-FRIENDLY, BUT HAS BEEN PROVEN TO REDUCE STRESS AND HELP WITH ANXIETY.. <u>PLUS</u> HAVING PLANT LIFE IN YOUR HOME CAN IMPROVE AIR QUALITY!!

Deciding what to cultivate isn't all about personal preference, but also about environmental limitations. For example, it would be extremely difficult to recreate the tropical climate needed for pineapple growth in a very cold snowy Canadian town. There are, however, a lot of very resilient vegetables and herbs, like cabbages, tomatoes, peppers and mint!!

REASONS TO INCLUDE YOUR FAMILY

1 WHEN IT COMES TO HELPING THE EARTH, THE MORE THE MERRIER! WE NEED ALL THE HELP WE CAN GET!!

2 BONDING WITH YOUR FAMILY IS IMPORTANT, AND BONDING OVER THE GROWTH OF A LIVING THING IS BEAUTIFUL! PLUS THINK OF THE POSSIBLE CONTESTS!!

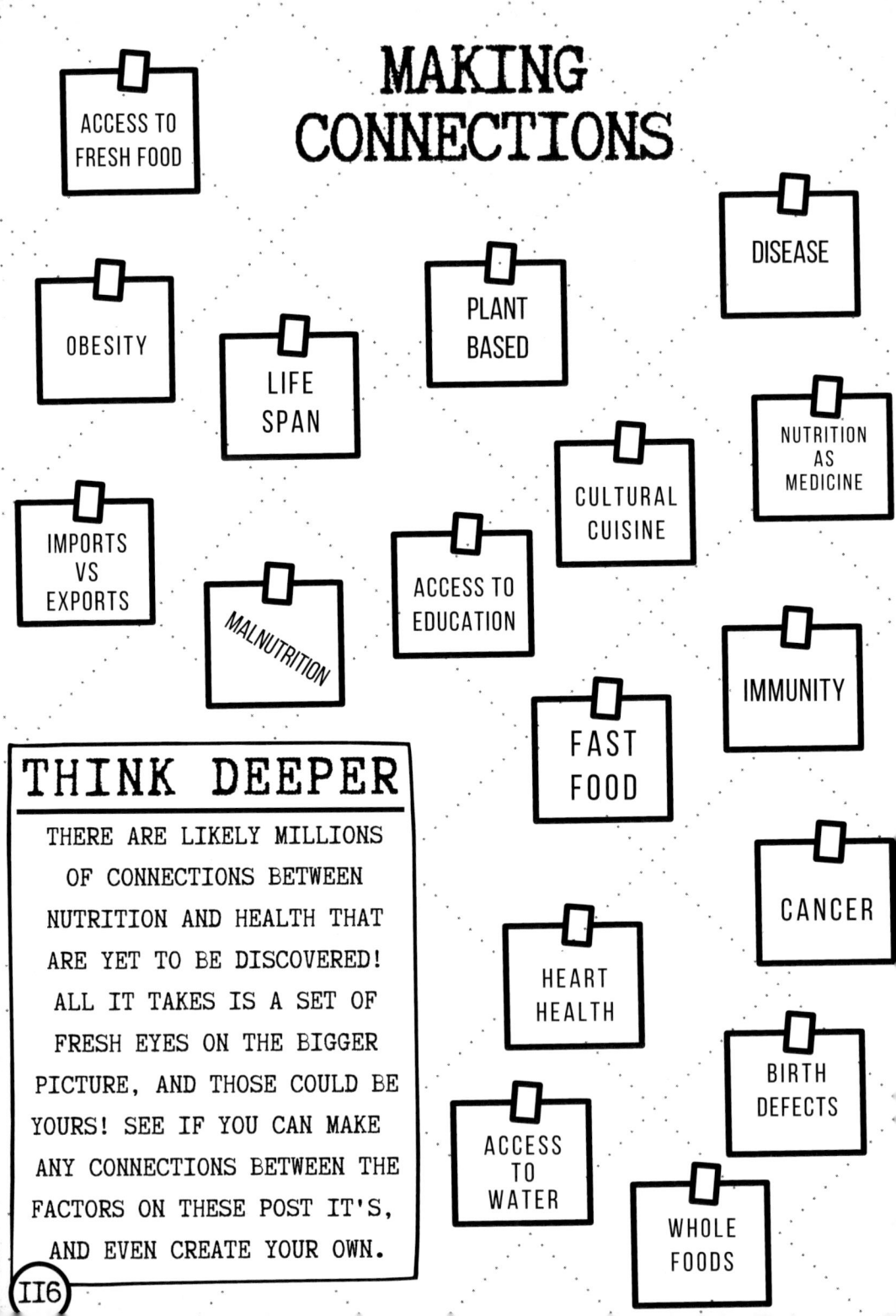

KEEP LEARNING

- STAY IN THE LOOP -

It takes commitment to stay on top of all of the new research in the field of nutrition; and while it is a commitment to your health, it is much better to STAY IN THE LOOP, than to spend hours & hours getting lost in all that new information. Invest your research time into specific subjects of nutrition that are personal to you, and find a few sources that you really trust to keep you informed. When choosing your sources, try to refer back to page 108 for help.

- OPEN UP YOUR WORLD -

The best way to STAY IN THE LOOP, and to keep learning & evolving, is to OPEN UP YOUR WORLD. Surround yourself with culture, new experiences & people, do so with open eyes and open ears, and never aim to <u>always</u> be the smartest in the room; not only will you always be learning, but you'll soon see that more comes from your experiences than just adventure for your tastebuds.

MOST IMPORTANTLY
HAVE CONVERSATIONS

BY NOW YOU KNOW THAT EVERYONE UNIQUE, WITH DIFFERENT BACKGROUNDS, TASTEBUDS & EXPERIENCES; SO TALK TO & CELEBRATE THE PEOPLE AROUND YOU!!

IT IS JUST AS IMPORTANT TO TEACH AS IT IS TO LEARN. THERE IS NO REASON <u>YOU</u> CAN'T BE A PART OF THE CONVERSATION IF YOU WANT TO BE.

UPCOMING BOOKS

KIDS IN THE KITCHEN

In this series, you will learn all the basics of the kitchen, giving you the tools you'll need to safely explore the joys of cooking!! This book includes:

- kitchen safety
- utensil use
- shelf life
- food & culture
- meal planning
- recipes
  - including no heat & guest recipes!

wasteNOT

The KEDO "wasteNOT" series aims to give you, your friends, and your family, 100's of ways to reduce your waste, and in turn, your Carbon Footprint. From your first garden, to gift ideas, doing your part to help keep the Earth healthy will never be so fun!! To have your wasteNOT idea featured in this series, on YouTube, or the KEDO platforms, (and with your parents' permission), submit it to us through our email or website!

SUPERFOODS & POWER POTIONS

After reading the 'Basics of Nutrition", you will have heard of these "superfoods", (see page 66).. and yes, they really do exist. Some are so yummy, they'll make you drool, some taste so bad, you'll need to pinch your nose & finish it superFAST, but with this collection of recipes from heroes all over the world, powering up will be a scrumptious breeze. Recipes include superFOCUS, superHEART and even healing powers!

!COME FIND US!

online
www.kedounion.com/kids

YouTube
SEARCH FOR OUR "KEDO KIDS" PLAYLIST!

kids@kedounion.com
EMAIL

instagram
@KedoUnion

sources & resources

Timmins, P.A., Wall, J.C. Bone water. Calc. Tis Res. 23, 1-5 (1977). https://doi.org/10.1007/BF02012759

Physico-chemical state of ions and water in living tissues and model systems. Ann. N.Y. Acad. Sci. 204 (1973)

Fernández, KS; de Alarcón, PA (December 2013). "Development of the hematopoietic system and disorders of hematopoiesis that present during infancy and early childhood". Pediatric Clinics of North America. 60 (6): 1273-89. doi:10.1016/j.pcl.2013.08.002. PMID 24237971.

Babcock, P. G., ed. 1976. Webster's Third New International Dictionary. Springfield, Massachusetts: G. & C. Merriam Co.

Vaughan, J. G., C. Geissler, B. Nicholson, E. Dowle, and E. Rice. 1997. The New Oxford Book of Food Plants. Oxford University Press.

From MDG's to SDGs. A new era for global public health 2016-2030" United Nations Sustainable Development Summit 2015. Sept 25-27, 2015. NYC, USA

Smolin, Grosvenor, Garfinkel; Wiley: Nutrition, Science & Application

Illness/Welness Continuum, Wellness Workbook 3rd Edition, by John Travis, MD, and Regina Sara Ryan, Celestial Arts, Berkeley. Copyright 1981, 1988, 2004 by John W. Travis. www.wellnessworkbook.com

Erin McLean, Bruno de Benoist, & Lindsay H. Allen;'Review of the Magnitude of Folate & Vitamin B-12 Deficiencies Worldwide'.

Diriba B. Kumssa, Edward J. M. Joy, E. Louise Ander, Michael J. Watts, Scott D. Young, Sue Walker & Martin R. Broadley; 'Dietary Calcium & Zinc Deficiency Risks are Decreasing but Remain Prevalent', 22 June, 2015

FAO, IFAD, UNICEF, WFP and WHO. 2019. The State of Food Security and Nutrition in the World 2019. Safeguarding against economic slowdowns and downturns. Rome, FAO. Licence: CC BY-NC-SA 3.0 IGO.

Gary Null, Ph.D.; The Complete Encyclopedia of Natural Healing: A Comprehensive A-Z Listing of Common & Chronic Illnesses and their Proven Natural Treatments, Sept., 2000
Frederic H. Martini, Ph.D., Kathleen Welch, M.D.; Fundamentas of Anatomy & Physiology, Fourth Edition, Applications Manual, 1997.

Food and Agriculture Organization of the United Nations, World Trade Organization; 'Trade and Food Standards', 2017.

Harvard Health Publishing, Harvard Medical School; Harvard Men's Health Watch: Understanding Acute and Chronic Inflammation, Published April, 2020

King, F.S. and Burgess, A.; Nutrition for Developing Countries, New York: Oxford University Press, 1993

sources & resources

World Health Organization, The Global Health Observatory - www.who.int

Food & Agriculture Organization of the United Nations - www.fao.org

Action Against Hunger - www.actionagainsthunger.org

Our World In Data - www.ourworldindata.org

Global Hunger Index - www.globalhungerindex.org

Human Development Index by United Nations

Ontario Ministry of Agriculture, Food and Rural Affairs

The Water in You: Water and the Human Body - USGS.gov, www.usgs.gov

University of Alberta, Faculty of Physical Education & Recreation. www.physedandrec.ualberta.ca

Fitness Tracker by Under Armour

NIH Database - https://ods.od.nih.gov/factsheets/Selenium-HealthProfessional/

Government of Canada - www.canada.ca

Food and Drug Administration - www.fda.gov

University of Cambridge, TLP Library - https://www.doitpoms.ac.uk

Try to fill in some of your own!